Praise for *Radical Compassion*

"Illuminating . . . Anyone hoping to gain a deeper understanding of themselves and advice for easing the burden of negative emotions will find this to be a helpful resource."

—*Publishers Weekly*

"*Radical Compassion* lays out a path of straightforward, accessible practices grounded in both modern brain science and ancient wisdom—with the soul and depth you'd expect from a world-class meditation teacher and psychologist. A masterpiece."

—Rick Hanson, PhD, author of *Resilient: How to Grow an Unshakable Core of Calm, Strength, and Happiness*

"A powerful book that will free you from shame, fear, and negative self-beliefs. You will feel wiser, happier, and kinder after reading it."

—Haemin Sunim, author of *Love for Imperfect Things* and *The Things You Can See Only When You Slow Down*

"Tara Brach has an uncanny ability to home in precisely on what we need in the moment, so we can meet that need from within. She teaches a simple but life-changing practice to bring presence and compassion to any moment of shame or longing or struggle, transforming our pain into love. This book is a treasure from one of the most important spiritual teachers of our time."

—Kristin Neff, PhD, author of *Self-Compassion: The Proven Power of Being Kind to Yourself*

PENGUIN LIFE

RADICAL COMPASSION

Tara Brach, PhD, is an internationally known teacher of mindfulness, meditation, emotional healing, and spiritual awakening. She is the author of *Radical Acceptance* and *True Refuge*, and her weekly podcasted talk and meditation is downloaded by over a million and a half people each month. Tara is the senior teacher and founder of Insight Meditation Center of Washington, DC. She lives in Great Falls, Virginia, with her husband and dog.

ALSO BY TARA BRACH

True Refuge:
Finding Peace and Freedom in Your Own Awakened Heart

Radical Acceptance:
Embracing Your Life with the Heart of a Buddha

Radical Compassion

LEARNING *to* LOVE YOURSELF *and* YOUR WORLD
with the PRACTICE *of* RAIN

TARA BRACH

life

PENGUIN BOOKS
An imprint of Penguin Random House LLC
penguinrandomhouse.com
A Penguin Life Book

First published in the United States of America by Viking,
an imprint of Penguin Random House LLC, 2019
Published in Penguin Books 2020

ISBN 9780525522836 (PAPERBACK)

THE LIBRARY OF CONGRESS HAS CATALOGED THE
HARDCOVER EDITION AS FOLLOWS:
Title: Radical compassion : learning to love yourself and your world with the
practice of RAIN / Tara Brach.
Description: New York : Viking, [2019] |
Identifiers: LCCN 2019011639 (print) | LCCN 2019015933 (ebook) |
ISBN 9780525522829 (ebook) | ISBN 9780525522812 (hardcover)
Subjects: LCSH: Mindfulness (Psychology) | Self-actualization
(Psychology) | Self-acceptance.
Classification: LCC BF637.M56 (ebook) | LCC BF637.M56 .B73 2019
(print) | DDC 158—dc23
LC record available at https://lccn.loc.gov/2019011639

Printed in the United States of America
9th Printing

Designed by Amanda Dewey

For Mia, and for all our children's children—

May your pure, bright hearts bring healing to our world

I live my life in widening circles
That reach out across the world.
I may not ever complete the last one,
But I give myself to it.

• RAINER MARIA RILKE

CONTENTS

PART III RAIN and Your Relationships

GUIDED REFLECTIONS, MEDITATIONS, AND REMEMBRANCES

PREFACE

LOVING OURSELVES INTO HEALING

Many years ago, I read a moving article by a hospice caregiver who had accompanied thousands of people during their final weeks. One phrase in particular has stayed with me. After countless hours listening to the thoughts of the dying, the caregiver summed up their greatest regret with these words: "I wish I'd had the courage to live a life true to myself."

I started asking myself questions like these: What does it mean to live true to yourself? Do you feel that your life is aligned with what matters to your heart? Are you living true to yourself—today? Right now? A few months later, I began asking the same questions of my meditation students.

What I found is that this regret of the dying is also true for many of the rest of us. My students tell me that being true to themselves means being loving, present, and authentic. They speak of being honest, serving others, serving the world. They talk about expressing their creativity, believing in their own worthiness, and working at what they love. And about having the strength to grow beyond their insecurities and to reconcile troubled relationships.

They also say that almost daily they lose sight of these aspirations and intentions. Instead, they get caught up in reactivity—self-judgment, blaming others, pettiness, selfishness, living on autopilot. As one student said, "Each day there's a big gap between what's possible and how I'm actually living my life. And with that comes an ever-lurking sense of personal failure."

I know that feeling of failure intimately. For many years, the "trance of unworthiness" kept me feeling deficient as friend and daughter, partner and parent. It fueled doubt about my capability as therapist and teacher. And when I faced severe physical illness, it initially triggered self-blame: "What did I do wrong to get so sick?"

Yet this very suffering—feeling deficient and disconnected—has also been my most fertile ground for waking up. It has led me to a spiritual path and practices that I cherish. And when I get stuck in painful emotions, it brings me to a repeating realization, an insight that has profoundly changed my life: *I have to love myself into healing.* The only path that can carry me home is the path of self-compassion.

It doesn't matter if I'm caught in anger, fear of failing at something important, a sense of self-doubt, or loneliness. And it doesn't matter if I'm facing yet again challenges to physical mobility and well-being. The healing medicine always has some flavor of care, compassion, or forgiveness. On some level, I'm telling myself, "Please, be kind." This turning toward loving presence is the gateway to living true to ourselves.

"Radical compassion" means including the vulnerability of this life—all life—in our heart. It means having the courage to love ourselves, each other, and our world. Radical compassion is rooted in mindful, embodied presence, and it is expressed actively through caring that includes all beings.

There's an image I love that shows mindfulness and compassion as inseparable dimensions of awakening. It depicts awareness as a bird with two wings: When both wings are unfurled in their fullness and beauty, the bird can fly and be free.

I'm writing this book to share a practice of radical compassion that brings alive the wings of mindfulness and compassion when we most need them. It helps heal and release the painful beliefs and emotions that keep us from living true to ourselves. This practice is called RAIN. The name is an acronym that stands for the four steps of Recognize, Allow, Investigate, and Nurture. Working with these four steps has given me—and can give you—a reliable way to find healing and freedom right where you are in the midst of emotional pain.

As you'll see, these steps are easy to learn, and they can be a lifeline in moments when you feel stressed, fearful, reactive, and confused. These same steps, revisited again and again, build internal resilience and trust in your own wise, awakening heart. They will help you respond to life in a way that expresses the truth and depth and spirit of who you are. This is the gift of RAIN: living from your full potential.

I was not the first to use the acronym RAIN. As some readers may already know, it was originally introduced as a meditation guide by the senior Buddhist teacher Michele McDonald in the 1980s, and since then it has been adopted and adapted in various ways by mindfulness teachers. Over the past fifteen years, I've evolved my own approach to RAIN, adding a step (N-Nurture) that directly awakens self-compassion. With this crucial emphasis, RAIN cultivates the synchronistic power of mindfulness and heartfulness—both wings of awareness. I've now shared this version with hundreds of thousands of people. The response has been tremendous, with people from around the world reporting how RAIN has brought a mindful, caring presence directly to the tangles of their daily lives, increasing their capacity for intimacy, releasing them from addictive behavior, empowering them in their work in the world, and supporting them in times of crisis. They tell me they can finally hold themselves with compassion and bring this same compassion to others. And they talk about the gift of inner freedom, of realizing who they are, beyond any story of self.

This book will develop your capacity for radical compassion. You'll learn to work with RAIN through a weave of stories and direct teaching, guided meditations, and many opportunities for self-reflection. You'll see how insights from modern neuroscience help explain the profound and enduring impact of RAIN. You'll also hear responses to the questions my students ask, and the many creative ways they've found to customize their practice. As we begin our journey together, here's a brief look ahead.

Part 1 is an overview of each step of RAIN. I'll offer examples that can help you to begin working with the steps right away. Even a few minutes with RAIN can interrupt the cutoff state I call "living in trance" and enable us to be more present with ourselves and others. Using RAIN, we can also begin to break through the various ways we say no to life, and to glimpse the true potential of our awakened heart.

Part 2 guides you in bringing RAIN to your inner life. Drawing on situations my students and I have worked on together, it describes how to refine and apply the four steps to a wide range of challenging circumstances, from shame and disabling fears to discovering your deepest longing. It also offers specific techniques for recruiting and cultivating your inner strengths.

Part 3 takes our journey into the field of relationships. These chapters include practices that awaken your capacity for forgiveness, help you to see past the mask of "unreal others" and wisely navigate conflict, unseen bias, and difference. In time, your deepening mindfulness and kindness will include all those you reflect on, all those whose lives you touch. You will discover the blessing of radical compassion, of loving without holding back.

. . .

I've had the privilege of witnessing countless people heal with the radical compassion that is nourished by RAIN. What strikes me again and again is how RAIN cultivates a trust in our own basic goodness and by extension helps us recognize and trust that same light shining through all beings. Seeing so many students, friends, and family discover this openhearted awareness, this reverence for life, nourishes my faith in our potential.

It also gives me hope for our world. From an evolutionary perspective, our species' brain development correlates with a growing capacity for self-awareness, rational thinking, empathy, compassion, and mindfulness. No question, our very human fears and grasping, combined with our cognitive ability, also make us the greatest danger on earth to ourselves and all other species. But we are not at the end of our evolutionary story. We have the tools that can awaken mindfulness and compassion in ourselves and guide us in relating wisely and lovingly with others.

Your dedication to awakening your heart is an essential part of the healing of our precious world. The global expressions of suffering—violence, the oppression of nondominant populations, the unsustainable and addictive consuming that threatens this earth—all arise out of fear and are rooted in feelings of separation and otherness. Radical compassion expresses the truth of our interdependence and mutual belonging. Living true to ourselves becomes, in its fullness, living true to our collective path of healing and freedom, our shared yearning for a peaceful, loving world.

Please remember and trust we're on this journey of awakening together. May you find true happiness and freedom on the path.

With loving blessings,
Tara

Radical Compassion

PART I

How Attention Heals

ONE

RAIN Creates a Clearing

Do not try to save the whole world or do anything grandiose. Instead, create a clearing in the dense forest of your life.

• MARTHA POSTLEWAITE

We all get lost in the dense forest of our lives, entangled in incessant worry and planning, in judgments of others, and in our busy striving to meet demands and solve problems. When we're caught in that thicket, it's easy to lose sight of what matters most. We forget how much we long to be kind and openhearted. We forget our ties to this sacred earth and to all living beings. And in a deep way, we forget who we are.

This forgetting is a part of being in trance—a partially unconscious state that, like a dream, is disconnected from the whole of reality. When we're in trance, our minds are narrowed, fixated, and usually immersed in thought. Our hearts are often defended, anxious, or numb. Once you recognize the signs of trance, you will begin to see it everywhere, in yourself and others. You are in trance when you are living on autopilot, when you feel walled off and separate from those around you, when you are caught up in feeling fearful, angry, victimized, or deficient.

The good news is that we all have the capacity to free ourselves.

When we are lost in the forest, we can create a clearing simply by pausing and turning from our clamoring thoughts to become aware of our moment-to-moment experience. I call this wakeful and immediate awareness "presence." It is also referred to as consciousness, spirit, Buddha nature, true nature, the awakened heartmind, and many other names. When we've reconnected fully to presence, we can open to what is going on inside us—the changing flow of sensations, feelings, and thoughts—without any resistance. This allows us to live our life moments with clarity and compassion. The shift from being lost in unconscious mental and emotional reactivity to inhabiting our full presence is an awakening from trance.

As we begin our journey together, the four steps of RAIN—Recognize, Allow, Investigate, Nurture—will be our tool for arriving in presence. *Simply put, RAIN awakens mindfulness and compassion, applies them to the places where we are stuck, and untangles emotional suffering.* It is easy to learn the basics, and you can begin to use the steps right away. RAIN creates a clearing in the dense forest, and in this clearing you can recover your full heart and spirit.

In this chapter, I'll walk you briefly through each step of RAIN and offer a simple form of the practice—a warm-up—that you can apply in everyday situations. But first, the story of an afternoon when I needed RAIN.

"NOT ENOUGH TIME"

My dense forest hums with a background mantra: *There's not enough time*. I know I'm not alone; many of us speed through the day, anxiously crossing tasks off the list. This often comes hand in hand with feeling beleaguered, annoyed at interruptions, and worried about what's around the corner.

My anxiety escalates when I'm preparing for an upcoming teaching event. I remember an afternoon some years ago when I was in last-minute mode. I was madly searching through my very disorganized electronic files, trying to find material for a talk I'd be giving that evening on loving kindness. Much like the files, my mind was stirred up and muddy. At one point, my eighty-three-year-old mother, who had come to live with my husband, Jonathan, and me, popped into my office. She started to tell me about an article she liked from *The New Yorker*. But seeing me glued to the computer screen (and probably frowning), she quietly placed the magazine on my desk and left. As I turned to watch her retreat, something in me just stopped. She often came by for a casual chat, and now I was struck by the reality that she wouldn't always be around for these companionable moments. And then I was struck again: Here I was, ignoring my mom and mentally scurrying around to compose a talk on love!

This wasn't the first time I was jarred by forgetting what mattered. During that first year my mom lived with us, I repeatedly felt squeezed by the additional demands on my time. Often when we had dinner together, I'd be looking for the break in the conversation when I could excuse myself and get back to work. Or we'd be on errands or going to one of her doctor's appointments, and rather than enjoying her company, I'd be fixated on how quickly we could get everything done. Our time together often felt obligatory: She was lonely, and I was the main person around. While she didn't guilt-trip me—she was grateful for whatever time I offered—I felt guilty. And then when I'd slow down some, I also felt deep sadness.

That afternoon in my office, I decided to take a time-out and call on RAIN to help me deal with my anxiety about being prepared. I left my desk, went to a comfortable chair, and took a few moments to settle myself before beginning.

The first step was simply to Recognize (R) what was going on inside me—the circling of anxious thoughts and guilty feelings.

The second step was to Allow (A) what was happening by breathing and letting be. Even though I didn't like what I was feeling, my intention was *not* to fix or change anything and, just as important, *not* to judge myself for feeling anxious or guilty.

Allowing made it possible to collect and deepen my attention before starting the third step: to Investigate (I) what felt most difficult. Now, with interest, I directed my attention to the feelings of anxiety in my body—a physical tightness, pulling and pressure around my heart. I asked the anxious part of me what it was believing, and the answer was deeply familiar: It believed I was going to fail. If I didn't have every teaching and story fleshed out in advance, I'd do a bad job and let people down. But that same anxiety made me unavailable to my mother, so I was also failing someone I loved dearly. As I became conscious of these pulls of guilt and fear, I continued to Investigate. Contacting that torn, anxious part of myself, I asked, "What do you most need right now?" I could immediately sense that it needed care and reassurance that I was not going to fail in any real way. It needed to trust that the teachings would flow through me, and to trust the love that flows between my mother and me.

I'd arrived at the fourth step of RAIN, Nurture (*N*), and I sent a gentle message inward, directly to that anxious part: "It's okay, sweetheart. You'll be all right; we've been through this so many times before . . . trying to come through on all fronts." I could feel a warm, comforting energy spreading through my body. Then there was a distinct shift: My heart softened a bit, my shoulders relaxed, and my mind felt more clear and open.

I sat still for another minute or two and let myself rest in this clearing, rather than quickly jumping back into work.

My pause for RAIN took only a few minutes, but it made a big difference. When I returned to my desk, I was no longer caught inside the story line that something bad was around the corner. Now that I wasn't tight with anxiety, my thoughts and notes began to flow, and I remembered a story that was perfect for the talk. Pausing for RAIN had enabled me to reengage with the clarity and openheartedness that I hoped to talk about that evening. And later that afternoon, my mom and I took a short, sweet walk in the woods, arms linked.

Since then, I've done a brief version of RAIN with anxiety countless times. My anxiety hasn't gone away, but something fundamental has changed. The anxiety doesn't take over. I don't get lost in the dense forest of trance. Instead, when I pause and then shift my attention from my story about getting things done to my actual experience in my body and heart, there's a spontaneous shift to increased presence and kindness. Often I'll keep working, but sometimes I decide to change gears, to step outside and play with my pup, make some tea, or water the plants. There's more choice.

OUR PATHWAY OUT OF TRANCE: TAKING A U-TURN

When I'm in the trance of busily speeding through the day, I'm typically lost in thoughts, disconnected from my body, and cut off from my heart. RAIN provides a way out of trance through what I call a "U-turn" in attention.

We are taking a U-turn whenever we shift our attention from an outward fixation—another person, our thoughts, or our emotionally driven stories about what's going on—to the real, living experience in our body. It's like being at a scary movie where we're totally gripped by the story on the screen and then suddenly become aware: *Okay, it's just a movie. I'm watching it with hundreds of other people. I can feel the seat under me, feel myself breathing.* And we're back again, aware of our own presence, grounded in our real life.

Only by purposefully bringing attention to our inner experience can we move from trance toward healing. We need to become aware of the circling anxious thoughts, the habitual tightness in our shoulders, the pressure from being in a rush. Then we can begin to turn from our stories—about someone else's wrongness, about our own deficiencies, about trouble around the corner—to directly feel our fears, hurts, and vulnerability, and ultimately the tender wakefulness of our heart. This all-important shift unfolds progressively through the steps of RAIN. But the key is, we have to first realize we're in trance!

AM I IN TRANCE OR IN PRESENCE?

In teaching about awareness, I often use an image created by Joseph Campbell: a circle with a line through it.

Above the line is everything we are conscious of, and below 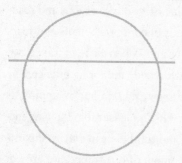 the line is everything outside our conscious awareness—a hidden world of fears, aversion, conditioning, and beliefs. To the degree that we're living below the line, we're in trance.

Being in trance is like being in a dream. We're unaware that there's a larger, living reality. And awakening from trance is like waking from a dream. We become self-aware, directly experiencing our inner life, the world we belong to, and the space of awareness itself. Living above the line is living in presence.

Presence has three primary characteristics: wakefulness, openness, and tenderness or love. Many spiritual traditions describe presence as an open, sunlit sky. When presence is full, like the sky it is luminous and boundless, and it provides warmth and nourishment for life. All kinds of weather systems pass through it—happiness, sorrow, fear, excitement, grief— but like the sky itself, presence can hold them all.

We've all touched presence. We're resting in presence in the moments before sleep when we become still and relaxed, listening to the rain on the roof. There's a background of presence when we gaze in wonder at a star-filled sky. We open to presence in gratitude for someone's unexpected kindness. We may never forget the presence we feel as we witness a birth or a death. Past and future recede, thoughts quiet, and we're aware of being right here, right now.

In contrast, trance encloses us in a virtual reality of thoughts and emotionally charged stories. We're trying to solve problems, satisfy desires, get rid of discomfort, or make our way to a future when things might be better. We are at the mercy of unconscious beliefs, feelings, and memories that drive our decisions and reactions to life. Not only that, but our unconscious wants and fears shape our deepest sense of who we are. When we're in trance, we usually feel separate or alone, threatened, and/or incomplete.

Our daily trance can feel ordinary and familiar, wrapping us in a cocoon of habit. It can carry us in pleasurable fantasy, immerse us in obsessive thinking, and tumble us in waves of painful emotion. But whatever the content of our trance, we are cut off from ourselves and cut off from our capacity to connect authentically with those around us. We're just not all there!

How do we know when we're in trance? We often don't know. But I've heard many people describe how they woke up to their particular versions of being under the line, in trance.

FLAGS OF TRANCE

- I realize I've just gone through a whole bag of trail mix.
- Everybody's the bad guy today—my kids, my boss, my partner—I'm finding fault with the world.
- I catch myself sizing up other men to see who's the most dominant.
- Even the small stuff feels like "just too much."
- I'm listening to someone and planning how to get outside for a cigarette.

- I lose an hour following links online.
- My neck starts hurting, and I realize my shoulders are up and knotted and that I've been anxious for hours.
- I notice the inner voice (my mother's) saying, "Can't you do anything right?"
- I'm walking through a store and suddenly realize I'm comparing my body with every other woman's I see.
- I'm rushing around trying to get things done, and I hurt myself or break something or make a stupid mistake.

Recognizing our flags helps us to step out of trance. For me, this means that when I catch myself anxiously rerunning my to-do list, or feeling guilty about letting someone down, I become more alert. These wake-up calls help bring into consciousness my fear of falling short and the physical tension I'm carrying. Then I can remember that my fearful beliefs aren't truth and that I have more choice as to how to spend my time.

TRANCE	PRESENCE
unconscious—below the line	conscious—above the line
asleep, in a dream	wakeful, lucid, aware
caught or possessed by emotions	emotions witnessed mindfully
dissociated	in contact with feelings
heart defended or numb	heart caring and tender
reactive to experiences	responsive to experiences
grasping or resisting	balanced, open, and discerning

Ask yourself, "Right now, what is my experience of presence?" or "Is there anything between me and presence?" Even these simple inquiries can alert you to trance and begin to awaken your awareness.

Or look back on your day and scan for the times when you were under the line. Can you identify some of the flags of trance for you? Sometimes in trance there's just enough consciousness to recognize that you're struggling, conflicted, shut down, or anxious. These wake-up calls let you know you need the healing—the sunlit sky—that is available above the line. This is when you call on RAIN.

LOVE SHINES THROUGH THE CLEARING

Four years after moving in with Jonathan and me, my mother was diagnosed with lung cancer. One afternoon six months later—about three weeks before her death—I sat by her bedside reading from a book of short stories we both love. She fell asleep as I was reading, and I sat there watching her resting easily. After some minutes, she woke up and mumbled, "Oh, I thought you'd be gone; you have so much to do." I leaned over, kissed her cheek, and continued to sit with her. She fell back to sleep, a slight smile on her lips.

I did have a lot to do. I always have a lot to do. I flashed on being too busy to pause and talk about that *New Yorker* article, and all those times I'd rushed through our shared dinners, felt dutiful about spending time together and guilty when I saw her walking outside alone. But my practice of RAIN had changed something. In our final years together, I was able to pause and really be there. I was there for making our supersized salads, for walking our dogs by the river, for watching the news, for chatting long after we'd finished a meal.

Twenty minutes later, my mother woke up again and whispered, "You're still here." I took her hand and she soon drifted off. I began crying silently, and something in her was attuned because she squeezed my hand. Oh, I'd miss her terribly. But my tears were also tears of gratitude for all the moments we lived together. And for the clearings that made this possible. On the day of her death, I was filled with immense sorrow and love, but no regrets.

Learning to create a clearing gives us our life. It is what opens us to the unfolding of radical compassion. When we're in trance, we can't really listen as our child shares excitedly about what happened at school. We can't pick up that a colleague is acting uptight because they are struggling with self-doubt and fear. We miss out on sunsets, chances to play, openings for intimacy, attunement to our own loneliness or longings. The practice of RAIN brings us above the line and lets us reconnect with presence and our naturally caring hearts.

REFLECTION: THE U-TURN TO PRESENCE

You might consider this a warm-up to practicing RAIN, something you can explore when you're stressed, rushing, and anxious. This

simple reflection can reconnect you with a sense of inner resourceful-
ness, self-compassion, and choice as to how you live your days.

—⊖—

Experiment with the U-turn at a time when you realize you've been lost in thought—perhaps obsessive worrying or planning, judging or fantasizing. Begin by pausing, sitting comfortably, and allowing your eyes to close. Take a few deep breaths, and with each exhale let go of any obvious tension in your mind and body.

Now shift your attention fully away from any remaining stories or thoughts, and notice your actual present-moment experience. What sensations are you aware of in your body? Are there any strong emotions present? Do you feel anxious or restless as you try to step out of your mental stories? Do you feel pulled to resume your activity? Can you simply stay right here, for just these few moments, and be with whatever is unfolding inside you? What happens if you intentionally regard your experience with kindness?

When you resume activity, notice if you sense any shift in the quality of your presence, energy, and mood.

QUESTIONS AND RESPONSES

Is it possible to experience presence when you're angry?

Yes! You are in a state of presence (above the line) when you're aware of the blaming thoughts and physical experience of anger. During these moments, in addition to the anger, there's a sense of witnessing the anger and some choice in how you respond. In contrast, you're in trance if you're lost inside the cycling thoughts and feelings of blame, with no sense of choice or control.

Do you have to follow a particular spiritual path to work with RAIN?

RAIN is a tool that can be used by anyone seeking to deepen self-understanding, self-compassion, compassion for others, and emotional healing and spiritual awakening. There is no requirement to hold a particular set of religious or spiritual beliefs. Whatever your beliefs, RAIN will enhance your direct experience of being awake and open, present and kind.

I have a regular mindfulness practice. Is RAIN a substitute for this? Or do they fit together?

They naturally weave together. The first two steps of RAIN, Recognize and Allow, are the foundation of mindful awareness and compassion. The second two steps, Investigate and Nurture, deepen mindfulness and directly activate compassion.

RAIN can be your tool for bringing mindfulness and compassion to a particular challenge. To explore this, continue with your regular mindfulness practice until you feel caught in a difficult emotion. In that moment, call on RAIN to guide you in systematically offering a mindful and kind attention directly to the emotional tangle. Once the tangle has loosened, return to your regular practice of moment-to-moment mindfulness.

In addition to including RAIN in the midst of a meditation sitting, you can pause anytime during the day when you feel stuck or challenged and call on RAIN to assist you.

Sometimes when I'm doing yoga, strong emotions like fear, anger, and self-doubt will come up. Can RAIN help at these times?

It's quite natural to experience strong emotions during a range of body-mind practices like yoga, tai chi, chi gung, breathwork, Reiki, guided imagery, and biofeedback. Many people have found that integrating a pause for RAIN opens the way to profound emotional healing and brings a powerful synergy to their path.

TWO

RAIN Says Yes to Life

The First Two Steps of RAIN

*Between the stimulus and the response there is a space,
and in that space is your power and your freedom.*

• VIKTOR FRANKL

The deepest transformations in our lives come down to some-thing very simple: We learn to respond, not react, to what is going on inside us. What happens, for example, when some-thing triggers our anger or anxiety? If our habit is to react by turning on ourselves, or by blaming or hurting other people, or by feeling victimized, we are adding to the suffering of trance. But if instead we awaken a mindful presence with the first two steps of RAIN—Recognize and Allow—we are on a path that frees our hearts.

HAVING TEA WITH MARA

One of the greatest myths from the Buddhist tradition shows how we can walk this path in the face of difficulty.

You may be familiar with images of the Buddha meditating all night long under the Bodhi tree until he experienced full liberation. The shadow god Mara (who represents the universal energies of greed, hatred, and delusion) tried everything he knew to make him fail—sending violent storms, beautiful temptresses, raging demons, and massive armies to distract him. Siddhartha met them all with an awake and compassionate presence, and as the morning star appeared in the sky, he became a Buddha, a fully realized being.

But this was not the end of his relationship with Mara!

In the five decades following his enlightenment, the Buddha traveled throughout northern India teaching all who were interested the path of presence, compassion, and freedom. In fields and forest groves, in villages and along riverbanks, farmers and tradesmen, townspeople and nobles, monks and nuns, all gathered to hear his wise teachings.

And as the Zen master Thich Nhat Hanh tells the story, Mara sometimes appeared as well. The Buddha's loyal attendant Ananda would spot him lurking furtively around the edge of a gathering and race to the Buddha with alarm. "Terrible news, the Evil One has returned! We've got to do something!" And each time, the Buddha would regard Ananda with great kindness. "Not so, Ananda," he'd reply. Then he'd stroll over to Mara and with a firm yet gentle voice say, "I see you, Mara. . . . Come, let's have tea." And the Buddha himself would serve Mara as an honored guest.

This is what's possible for us. Just imagine that Mara appears in your life as a surge of fear about failure, or hurt about another's neglect or disrespect. Now, what if your response were to pause and say, "I see you, Mara"—Recognizing. And "Let's have tea"—Allowing. Instead of avoiding your feelings, instead of lashing out in anger or turning on yourself with self-judgment, you are responding to life with more clarity and graciousness, kindness and ease. By taking these first two steps of RAIN, you have entered the path of freedom.

I consider this story of the Buddha good news for all of us. Even for the Buddha, the painful energies of Mara continued to arise. We're not the only ones who have to keep reengaging with storms of confusion, with conflicting desires, with arrows of fear or hurt or anger. And we have a liberating practice that can awaken us in the midst!

Ask yourself, "When has Mara recently appeared?" What would it be like at one of these times to say, "I see you, Mara. . . . Let's have tea"?

"NO" IS A HABIT

In inviting Mara to tea, the Buddha was saying yes to the present moment and yes to all of life.

In contrast, our habitual ways of saying no—of resisting or avoiding our experience—create more suffering. Consider what happens when Mara appears in the shape of fear, hatred, anger, or hurt. Our mind says no by immediately assuming that something is wrong, finding something or someone to blame, and trying to eliminate the problem. Our body says no by tensing or numbing; our heart says no by becoming defensive or closing down. Meanwhile, our behaviors say no when we lash out or withdraw or become preoccupied. And while we might be somewhat aware of our "no," for the most part we are below the line, lost in our unconscious efforts to control life.

Saying yes is unfamiliar and disorienting and feels potentially risky. When we perceive a threat, our primal conditioning is to contract and say no. In workshops, I often ask students to reflect on a difficult situation and then encourage them to watch the many different ways their body and mind resist the raw emotions going on inside them. They see, often with sadness, how their efforts to protect themselves are actually adding more pain to their lives.

One man, who had been bullied as a child, now had a critical supervisor who regularly threatened him with poor reports. As he replayed a recent confrontation, he could feel his stomach clenching in fear and his heart pounding. Instead of taking time afterward to open to his own experience (saying yes), he'd go right into blaming himself for feeling intimidated and mentally rage against his supervisor. Then he'd plunge back into activity, moving paperwork along faster while making more errors and communicating less clearly. His "no" perpetuated a familiar sense of himself as deficient and victimized.

An older woman who was estranged from her adult son traced her unconscious "no" to his occasional emails. She'd read his terse message, ask herself tearfully, "What did I do to deserve this?" and then begin to obsess about her daughter-in-law, whom she blamed for the problem. Inevitably, she realized, her resentment toward her daughter-in-law would leak into her return email. For her, "no" kept her trapped in feeling disliked and rejected.

Whatever form our "no" takes, it is a way of tensing against reality and trying to avoid the raw pain of emotional suffering.

But "no" can also become a flag that tells us we're in trance and need to deepen our attention. The more quickly we become aware of our "no," the better we can respond to Mara. The difficult situations that evoke a habitual "no" are perfect opportunities to experiment with the profound "yes" that is expressed by Recognize and Allow, our entry into RAIN.

WHEN MARA IS ANGRY

Roger, a top executive at an IT company, had a reputation for being impatient, irritable, and lightning quick to pounce on anyone who fell short on the job. He was even harder on his family. He'd rage at his teenage sons for dishes in the sink, loud music, or arriving home late. He'd lash out at his wife when she didn't do things exactly his way. Roger was caught in a reactive "no."

Finally, at his wife's insistence, Roger went to see a psychologist, who recommended meditation as a way to become more mindful and less reactive, and he became a regular at my weekly classes. After several months, Roger joined a daylong workshop on healing difficult emotions and asked to speak with me during the lunch break. He told me he had been meditating ten to twenty minutes a day but that his temper was still out of control. "I hate myself for losing it. I hate who I become," he said with disgust. "But it keeps happening again and again."

We found a quiet spot, and I introduced Roger to the *R* (Recognize) and the *A* (Allow) of RAIN. These ways of paying attention were already familiar to him from meditation class. Recognizing and Allowing—noticing what's happening in the present moment and, without judgment, letting it be—are the foundation of mindfulness. But now I would show him how to apply them directly to his habitual reactions.

We began by focusing on an incident from earlier in the week. A staff member had arrived at a meeting with an incomplete report, and Roger had exploded, berating him in front of the group. I suggested he close his eyes and follow his breath for a few moments, just as he did when he sat down to meditate. Once he'd collected his attention, I asked him to bring to mind the most upsetting part of the situation and then to ask himself the key question for the Recognition step: *What is happening inside me?* I guided him as he sat with his eyes closed: "Just witness the whole mix of thoughts, feelings, and sensations . . . and note what stands out. You might mentally whisper to yourself, 'Blaming . . . anger, anger,' or name the feelings in your body: 'heat . . . pressure . . . exploding.'" He was quiet for a few moments and then nodded.

Now I introduced the step of Allowing by suggesting a second key question: *Can I be with this?* or *Can I let this be?* Again I guided him. "With Allowing, you're agreeing to pause . . . to stay and feel your direct experience, even though it's really uncomfortable . . . even though you'd do almost anything not to feel it. See if you can whisper yes to the experience . . . and pause, letting whatever is there be as it is. That doesn't mean you're saying these feelings and thoughts are okay. You're just saying yes to the reality that they are here right now." I noticed he was hardly breathing, so I added, "It can really help to be mindful of your breath . . . your breath will help you stay present with the feelings in your body."

Once I saw he was breathing more fully, I waited about ten

seconds and then suggested he take a few more conscious breaths and open his eyes. He looked at me for a moment and raised his brows quizzically. "That's it? Name anger and—just like we tell the kids—count to ten?!?" We both laughed.

"Well, not quite, but try it out," I said. "Of course, you won't be closing your eyes if you're with other people, and there will probably be times when you forget and just get mad. But keep trying to remember, note what's going on inside, and Allow . . . breathe with your feelings . . . and sure, count to ten!"

Roger was game and curious. I told him his daily meditation practice would support his efforts to apply Recognize and Allow, and I invited him to email to tell me how it was going. As we parted, I said, "You can do this . . . and it will make a real difference." He gave me a thumbs-up.

WHAT YOU PRACTICE GETS STRONGER

I like to tell students the story of a man who went to a mindfulness retreat because his therapist said he'd feel better if he learned to meditate. The retreat turned out to be a real roller coaster. Yes, there were moments of calm, but he also plunged deeply into fear, anger, and grief. The next time he saw his therapist, he told him he'd suffered horribly. "How could you have promised I'd feel better?" Nodding sagely, the therapist replied, "You are feeling better . . . you're feeling your fear better, feeling your anger better, feeling your grief better!"

This always gets a laugh of recognition. Mindfulness meditation, the Recognize and Allow of RAIN, trains us to wake up out of distracting thoughts and make the U-turn, bringing a full, embodied attention to our moment-to-moment experience. We inevitably encounter everything we've been avoiding—the loneliness, hurts, and fears. And yet if we practice regularly, we discover that we can maintain a balanced, openhearted presence in the midst of the storm.

Thanks to current understandings of neuroplasticity, we now know that our brains can change throughout our lives. This means that even the most deeply rooted and harmful habits can be deconditioned. The phrase that sums this up is this: "Neurons that fire together, wire together." Our habits are sustained by repeating patterns of thoughts, feelings, and behaviors that have created and reinforced neural networks in our brain. By changing our patterns of thinking, feeling, and behaving, we can change these neural networks.

Many research studies have shown that mindfulness directly and positively impacts the structure and function of the brain. If we go into trance when we encounter stress—rushing around, worrying, judging—we reinforce the fear-based ruts in our mind. If instead we become mindful in times of stress, learning to pause and to Recognize and Allow our experience, something different is possible. Instead of reacting from our passing wants and fears, we can respond to our circumstances from a deeper intelligence, creativity, and care. This creates new patterning, new neural pathways in the brain that correlate with true well-being and peace.

The more you say yes to experience, the more the openness and presence of that "yes" will be embodied in living cells and shape your entire life experience.

RECOGNIZE AND ALLOW: A CLOSER LOOK

I introduced the steps of Recognize and Allow in chapter 1, but I want to say more here because these core elements of mindfulness are the foundation of RAIN.

Recognition starts the minute you focus your attention on whatever thoughts, emotions, feelings, or sensations you are experiencing right now. The key question here is this: "What is happening inside me?" See if you can take the perspective of a non-judging witness, and be curious! Take some time to notice whatever attracts your attention. There may be distressing thoughts, anxious feelings, hurt, confusion, or sorrow. Try to let go of any preconceived ideas and just listen in a kind, receptive way to your body and heart. You don't have to search. Simply become still and notice whatever is going on.

Sometimes you'll discover a whole swirl of experiences: confusion, anger, racing thoughts, anxiety. That's fine, just note any part of the cluster that stands out. There are other times when you may start out feeling numb or empty. In fact, these are emotional states, too. Simply name them: "empty," "numb."

Recognizing is the first step of awakening from trance. It may take only a few moments, but it is crucial. You're lifting your head above the waves of fear or anger; you're becoming a witnessing presence.

Allowing, the next step, asks you to "let be" whatever thoughts, emotions, feelings, or sensations you have just recognized. You initiate it by gently asking, "Can I be with this?" or "Can I let this be?" It's natural to feel resistance at this point—you wish some of those feelings would go away! Allowing can include the reality of your "no"—the fact that you really hate the way you're feeling.

Pause as the thoughts and emotions continue to unfold, without trying to control them or doing anything to resolve them. You may feel a strong urge to start analyzing and fixing things. You need to let that be as well. This is a time to let your awareness include everything that is going on inside you.

TWO KEY QUESTIONS OF MINDFULNESS

Ask yourself, "What is happening inside me?"

Now ask, "Can I be with this?" or "Can I let this be?"

Many students I work with help themselves "let be" by mentally whispering an encouraging word or phrase. You might feel the grip of fear or the swelling of deep grief and whisper yes. You might say, "This too" or "It's okay."

There are degrees of Allowing. At first, you may feel you're just going through the motions, "putting up" with unpleasant sensations. Or you may realize you've made a secret bargain—"I'll say yes to shame, and it will magically disappear." Yet even simply whispering yes begins to give you a sense of more space, more room for what is there. Your entire being is not so rallied in resistance. As you continue to practice, your defenses will ease up. You may feel a physical sense of yielding or relaxing and opening to waves of experience.

While Allowing doesn't necessarily reduce unpleasantness,

it radically shifts our relationship to pain in a way that reduces suffering. Imagine the difference between pouring a cup of dye into a sink full of water and pouring the same amount into a lake. Allowing expands us in a way that enables us to include, not fight, physical and emotional pain. Psychologists call this "affect tolerance."

Remembering this potential for healing helps you say yes to the reality of this moment. Together, Recognizing and Allowing enable a shift from a constricting trance to a more awake, spacious presence that can eventually include all of life. It is from this mindful awareness that you will discover fresh, creative, and more compassionate responses to life's challenges.

THE POWER OF YES

After several months, Roger emailed me a progress report. He'd been meditating before work each morning, and he found those times of stillness to be very calming and centering. What happened later in the day was less predictable. According to his calculations, when his anger was triggered, he managed to pause about one in four times. Sometimes the Recognizing and Allowing defused only a bit of his anger, and he still lashed out in ways he regretted. But at other times, it was starting to make a difference. His email ended with this story:

> I met with one of my project managers last Monday. He admitted his team was behind schedule on one of our major projects, that he had personally let a few things fall between the cracks.

I almost let loose on him, but remembered to stop . . .
to breathe, to ask what was happening, to name "anger"
and to let it be there. He was telling me how there was no
way around late delivery. Well, there I was, pausing,
breathing, and something in me started shifting because
instead of focusing on him screwing up, I was taking in
how dedicated, how honest this guy was. How thoughtful.
So I surprised both of us and said, "Look I know you're
doing the best you can."

He suddenly had tears in his eyes. That's when he
told me his wife had been diagnosed with stage-4 breast
cancer, that (like me) he has two teens, that it's been really tough.

Tara, we hugged, both of us with tears. A few
months ago, I would have unwittingly added to this
man's burden. And there we were hugging. It was one
of my saddest and best moments . . . it was like I had
found my way back to being a real human being.

Our deeply grooved habits of "no," our angry reactivity,
anxious worry, defensiveness, addictive behavior, and self-
blame, keep us from living true to ourselves. When we interrupt these habits with a mindful, allowing presence, we begin
to access our full human potential. This is the power and freedom inherent in "yes." It may help us end a prolonged conflict
and find a way to reconciliation. We may become able to speak
a difficult truth that has kept us from authenticity. We may let
go of overconsuming or oversleeping and live in a more healthy
way. Whatever the pattern of "no," practicing these first steps
of RAIN opens up the possibility for change.

When we encounter strong emotions, we often need to deepen mindfulness and self-compassion by moving on to the second two steps of RAIN, Investigate and Nurture. This is when having tea with Mara becomes lively and profoundly transformative! As you will see in chapter 3, the full practice of RAIN is critical in healing more deeply entrenched patterns.

REFLECTION: SAYING YES— AWAKENING MINDFULNESS

Take a few moments to sit quietly, collecting your attention by resting in the movement of your breath.

Bring to mind a situation that elicits a moderately strong emotional reaction of hurt, anger, fear, or shame (not one that might trigger trauma). It might involve a conflict within your family or with friends, an addictive behavior, or something difficult at work. Review that situation as if you were watching a movie until you get to the part that most activates strong emotions. Freeze the frame, and deepen your attention to whatever is going on that most disturbs you.

Ask yourself, "What is happening inside me?" and notice whatever feelings are most painful or intense.

Now, become aware of your attitude toward those feelings, all the ways you might be saying no to your experience. Are you thinking something is wrong, this shouldn't be happening, wishing it would go away, blaming yourself, blaming another— trying to change it or push it away? To experiment, send the word and energy of "no" directly into the place inside that most distresses you. Sense what happens to your body, heart, and mind when you reject what you're feeling. And notice if you often feel this way, if it seems to be a familiar part of yourself.

Now take a few full breaths. Then remind yourself again of the most difficult part of this situation and recall the feelings that are most painful. But this time, ask yourself, "Can I be with this?" Or alternately, "Can I let this be?" Sense that you have the space of awareness to include everything you've discovered, that you can fully allow it to be as it is. You can even say yes to the parts of you that are saying no and resisting what's happening.

Experiment by directing the word and energy of "yes" to whatever you are feeling most intensely. What does it feel like in your body when you say yes? How does "yes" affect your heart? Your mind? Let the "yes" be as full and unconditional as possible. What is your sense of your own being when you are saying yes?

Imagine the days and weeks to come. What would it be like if this situation arises again and you could name the difficult emotions, pause fully, and Allow them to be as they are? What possibilities might open up if you could pause and say yes to your inner life?

QUESTIONS AND RESPONSES

I'm concerned about saying yes when I've hurt someone, or when someone's hurt me. Isn't it important to say no to harmful behavior?

When you are saying yes, you are honestly acknowledging and opening to the reality of the present moment—your actual feelings and sensations. But you are in no way saying yes to harmful behaviors—your own or others'. If someone has been emotionally abusive and you say yes to your feelings of fear or anger, your "yes" does not include what that person has said or done. In fact, when you recognize and allow your inner experience, you'll find you can say no and set boundaries with greater courage and clarity.

But won't saying yes to my anger just inflame me more, make it more likely that I'll take it out on others?

Saying yes to anger—to the energetic heat and explosiveness in your body—is different from saying yes to the content of your angry thoughts. "Yes" to the energy of anger is not a confirmation of the "rightness" of thoughts. We are not agreeing that "yes, so-and-so really is bad or wrong," or "yes, I'm going to get back at him." We are simply acknowledging the reality of our anger. In fact, if our habit has been to lash out when we're hurt, saying yes enables us to pause and make the U-turn, staying present with our experience instead of reacting. In that pause, we might find what is buried under the anger. And, like Roger, we might also discover that we can choose other ways to respond. We are no longer trapped in an old pattern of hurt and blame.

When I'm judging myself for being a "bad" person, saying yes feels as if I were just confirming that I'm really flawed.

Just as with angry thoughts, when there are judging thoughts, "yes" simply Recognizes and Allows them to be there. It in no way affirms that the judgment itself ("I'm bad") is the truth. Like working with anger, when you Recognize and Allow judging, it becomes possible to make the U-turn and uncover the fear or shame that often accompanies the judgment you're feeling. This brings you above the line. You are increasingly able to respond to your own inner critic with more perspective, wisdom, and compassion.

What if saying yes—Recognizing and Allowing— makes my fear or shame even more intense? What if they are too much to handle?

Every emotion has an arc—it arises, peaks, and passes—unless we are continuously fueling it with thoughts. You may connect with an emotion when it is just arising and, by saying yes, Allow it to express its full intensity. If this is tolerable, it serves healing: The emotion is free to naturally arise and pass, and you are strengthening your capacity to rest in an open, witnessing presence. But if you feel that the intensity might be overwhelming, then this is not the time to say yes. The following chapters (particularly chapter 6, on fear) will show you many ways to seek support, strengthen your resilience, and develop other resources to rely on before you return to the practice of RAIN.

THREE

RAIN Reveals Your True Self

Steps Three and Four of RAIN

*Life is this simple: we are living in a world that is
absolutely transparent and the divine is shining
through it all the time. This is not just a nice story or
a fable, it is true.*

• THOMAS MERTON

In the mid-1950s, a new highway in Bangkok was routed through an ancient temple, and the monks were forced to relocate a massive clay statue of the Buddha that had been loved and venerated for many generations. A crane was brought in, but as they began to lift the Buddha, its huge weight shifted, and the clay began to crack. They quickly lowered the statue to the ground and, knowing a storm was coming, covered it with a tarp.

Later that evening, the abbot went to inspect the damage and make sure the statue wasn't getting wet. As he shone his flashlight under the tarp, he noticed a gleam of reflected light coming from the largest crack. When he looked more closely, he wondered if there was something underneath the thick clay. He ran to wake the other monks, and together, with chisels and hammers, they began chipping along the cracks. The gleam became brighter and brighter, until finally, after long hours of work, the monks stepped back and stared in awe at the sight before them: a Buddha of solid gold.

Historians believe that several hundred years earlier, the temple monks themselves had covered the statue with clay. Anticipating an attack by a neighboring army, they hoped to protect their precious Buddha from being looted or destroyed. The monks were all killed in the ensuing battle, but the Buddha survived intact.

When monks today share this story, they say that in the face of threats or challenges each of us has a habitual way of covering the gold. Our suffering comes when we identify with our protective covering and forget the loving awareness that is intrinsic to our being.

REMEMBERING THE GOLD

I read about the Golden Buddha a month or so after my first husband and I agreed to end our marriage. Because Alex and I had shared a spiritual practice for ten years, we'd expected to navigate divorce with friendship and respect. Yet here we were, caught in a hostile standoff over finances, child-care schedules, and many other details of creating two households. We were both seeing red, not gold!

Hoping that we could get past some of the bitterness, I'd

postponed telling Narayan, our five-year-old son, about our plans to separate. But now, with the image of the Golden Buddha in my mind, I started to see our blame and mistrust as clay coverings. That helped me remember the way Alex adored our son, his healing hands, how wonderful he was with plants and animals and small children. It helped me remember the love still there beneath my own fear and anger.

Over the next few days, the image of the Golden Buddha kept arising, and each time I felt more at peace with the reality that this was a tough season but that we'd come through, friendship intact.

One evening about a week later, I shared the story of the Golden Buddha with Narayan. Then I told him his dad and I wouldn't be living together anymore and explained how we'd both still love and care for him. His first response was "Okay," and then after some thoughtful moments he added, "But you still love each other, right?" I was able to say yes truthfully and really feel it. "Loving is the gold," I told him, "and that doesn't change."

If I could have fast-forwarded twenty-seven years, I'd have seen Alex looking on joyfully as Narayan and his wife, Nicole, cuddled with their new baby girl. I'd have seen myself walking on the beach, little Mia wrapped on my chest, with my husband, Jonathan, at my side. All of us are radiating gold.

WHO ARE WE, REALLY?

I often refer to our protective coverings as our "ego space suit." This space suit is made of all the strategies and defenses we develop to meet our needs for safety, approval, and love as we navigate through the hurts and conflicts of our families and culture. But as necessary as some of these defenses may be, they can also create suffering. When we cover over our innocence and purity, our vulnerability and tenderness, we lose sight of our essential being. Our identity becomes linked to our ego space suit, and we forget the gold.

If we widen our lens, we can see that this narrowing of identity is a natural part of our evolutionary unfolding. The primary activity of every living creature is to cling to life and avoid threats. We have a membrane or scales or skin or shell to protect us. We have reflexes and skills and strategies to make our way. Our brains are designed to perceive separateness and react to danger. When we humans emerged as life-forms on this planet, we were already organized around a wanting, fearful self and by extension around the small group or tribe we belonged to. But our story doesn't end here.

Because we are *Homo sapiens sapiens* (beings who know that they know), we are self-aware. The most recently evolved part of our brain, the prefrontal cortex, gives us our capacity to witness and feel compassion for whatever's going on inside us—and in others. As neuroscientists have discovered, learning to deepen our attention with meditation activates the parts of the brain that correlate with self-awareness. We can become aware of our unconscious fears and limiting beliefs; we can recognize how our unmet needs keep us armored or grasping. And we can begin to see how the whole sense of who we are has been confined and obscured by these ego coverings.

The mindfulness and compassion of RAIN allow us to

awaken from this imprisoning trance right in the middle of our daily lives. Each time we bring a gentle RAIN to the thick clay of our covering, it becomes slightly more transparent as our fear and grasping dissolve. Increasingly, the light of our gold shines through.

THE SECOND TWO STEPS OF RAIN: INVESTIGATE AND NURTURE

Sophia's world had collapsed when her boyfriend broke up with her at the beginning of her junior year of college. She and Zach had been together since freshman year, and Sophia had assumed they'd be life partners. He was everything she wanted—caring, bright, funny, and, when she was insecure, totally affirming. But now he was with someone else. Overwhelmed by anxiety and depression, she fell behind in her work and, on her counselor's advice, withdrew from school for the semester.

After being at home and working with a therapist for a number of months, Sophia had days when she felt more calm and hopeful. But then she'd imagine going back to school and be flung into panic. There she'd be facing all the stressors alone and, worse, running into Zach and his girlfriend. After Sophia spent a day shut in her bedroom, her mother—a regular at my Wednesday night class—asked if I would see her.

At first Sophia responded politely but briefly to my questions. But when I asked about her special interests at school, she began to tell me about her internship at an inner-city clinic for troubled youth and immediately came to life. She'd been teaching the kids yoga, she said, and co-leading a group on the basics of emotional intelligence. "I love being with them," she told me, "even when they're difficult. I get that if they're causing trouble, it's because they're hurting." She added wistfully, "I miss them more than anything else about being at college."

Then Sophia slumped, her eyes downcast. "I sometimes get really anxious; parties are just torture. I'm nervous around my professors, so they probably think I'm ignoring them, and I'm always obsessing about the next paper or exam. . . . I'm afraid that when I go back, it's going to get worse again." Then she added, "It's like without Zach, I've lost my safety net."

When I began to introduce RAIN, Sophia easily Recognized the self-critical voice in her head that took over when she thought about Zach: "I saw his girlfriend on Facebook . . . she is petite and blond and"—she gestured at her belly—"I probably put on ten pounds since we broke up. That voice tells me he never really loved me, he was just trying to be a hero . . . to save poor, pathetic me." She started to tear up and then impatiently dabbed at her eyes.

"Sophia," I said gently, "for now, can you name what this voice is saying as 'critical thoughts' and then just let them be there for a few minutes?" She nodded, and I explained that this step was called Allowing. We've Recognized our feelings, sensations, and thoughts, and we've stopped pushing them away or fighting them.

Then, after a pause, I guided Sophia into Investigate, the *I* of RAIN. "Now try to go inside your body—under your thoughts—and notice what you're most aware of."

"It's dark and heavy in there," she said, "and tight—squeezing."

"Can you tell me where that dark, heavy, tight feeling is the worst?" One hand immediately went to her heart, and I invited her to keep it there. "If that dark, heavy, tight place could communicate, what would it be expressing?"

After some moments of silence, Sophia said, "I see a little girl . . . she's me . . . crouched inside the darkness."

"Can you tell what she is believing?"

After a long pause, Sophia said, "That they will see something's wrong with her, she's bad in some way . . . and then they will stop loving her."

"Sophia, what's it like right now for you to sense this young part of yourself who's so lonely, so afraid of losing love?" Now Sophia put her face in her hands and began weeping. When she quieted, I gave her some tissues and water.

After a long while, she spoke. "She's just a child . . . she didn't do anything wrong . . . it's so, so sad."

I nodded and asked, "What does she most need from you?"

Sophia took a deep breath and then sighed. "She wants me to see her and know she's there . . . she wants to know that I care no matter what."

We were now about to move into the *N* of RAIN, Nurturing. I asked Sophia to take a few moments to breathe and then to call on her wisest, kindest self—the part of her that was able to see that little girl and feel her sadness and tenderness.

"Some people think of this part as their 'high self' or 'future self,'" I explained. "Maybe you experienced this wise and kind place when you were with the children at the clinic, so interested in them, caring about them."

Sophia opened her eyes and spoke softly. "It's true . . . that's how I feel sometimes—those kids are so young . . . having such a hard time . . . and it's not their fault." She paused. "I like that way of putting it . . . my future self."

She closed her eyes again, and we continued: "Sophia, now try placing your hand on your heart, and just as you might comfort one of those children, send care from your future self to your own younger self . . . and try calling her by her name."

A few moments later, she began to pat her heart slowly and gently. Then she whispered, "I'm here, Sophia, I want to be with you, I'm sorry it's so hard. I care. . . . I really care."

After a minute or so, I could see her breath become deep and full, and a few moments later she opened her eyes. I asked her how she was feeling. "When I comforted her, something shifted. I actually feel lighter—sad and light and more relaxed. Just now when I was sitting quietly, I felt more like . . . myself . . . who I want to be."

In our next meeting, I would tell Sophia the story of the Golden Buddha and how we get caught in the protective coverings and forget our goodness. But for now I gave her a simple assignment—to practice RAIN whenever that self-critical voice started in on her, judging and stirring up anxiety. It didn't matter how long she practiced. What mattered was making the U-turn—turning from her thoughts to Investigate what was going on inside her body and then offering compassion to whatever she found.

As she was leaving, Sophia said, "The only way I can imagine returning to school is if my future self goes in my place."

I laughed. Then I shared one of my favorite things about RAIN: "The more you Nurture yourself, the more you'll find you're living from your future self—the best of who you are."

"AFTER THE RAIN": GLIMPSING THE GOLD

After completing the steps of RAIN and sitting quietly for a short time, Sophia had felt more like herself, who she wanted to be. Those moments of resting and sensing the fullness of our own presence are what I call "After the RAIN." Just as there's freshness and clearing after a real rain, the first fruits of RAIN often appear right after we complete the four steps. Yet in our busy lives, it's all too easy to miss these precious moments. Instead of moving on immediately, we need to pause and rest in presence. Then we may notice that our sense of who we are has enlarged. We're no longer inside some limiting story, identified with a fearful or deficient self. We become aware of our natural openness, wakefulness, and tenderness. This is a precious taste of the gold, of our basic goodness.

For Sophia, connecting with this openhearted presence was the beginning of trusting herself. After she returned to college, she wrote me several emails. One began, "I used to think Zach was 'my safety net.' Now I realize my future self is always there to hold me." Then she went on to tell me about a nine-year-old girl at the clinic where she was interning. The girl had been abused in a foster home, and initially she wouldn't talk or even make eye contact with the staff. But then, on Sophia's third visit, the little girl asked her when she was coming back. "I told her next week, and then I asked her if we could have a good-bye hug. She nodded shyly and was pretty stiff, but when we hugged, I knew she didn't want to let go."

. . .

There's a calling within each of us to connect with the gold and live from the gold. We want to manifest our true nature, whether we call it our future self, high self, awakened heart, Buddha nature, Great Spirit, Christ consciousness, or the Divine. While identifying with the ego coverings is a universal part of our evolutionary path, the awakening of radical compassion frees us from this confining trance. RAIN can guide us home to the luminous and loving awareness that is our essence, and we can live from that compassionate presence. In part 2, we'll explore how to bring a healing RAIN directly to the places of fear and woundedness that most often block this inner radiance.

In the chapters to come, you'll also find suggestions for adapting your RAIN practice to a wide variety of situations. Here is a summary of the foundational steps that you can return to for review at any point.

MEDITATION: RAIN STEP-BY-STEP

Sitting quietly, close your eyes and take a few full breaths. Bring to mind a current situation in which you feel stuck, one that elicits a difficult reaction, such as anger or fear, shame or hopelessness. It may be a conflict with a family member, a chronic sickness, a failure at work, the pain of an addiction, a conversation you now regret. Take some moments to enter the experience—visualizing the scene or situation, remembering the words spoken, sensing the most distressing moments. Contacting the charged essence of the story is the starting place for exploring the healing presence of RAIN.

R: *Recognize What Is Happening*

As you reflect on this situation, ask yourself, "What is happening inside me right now?" What sensations are you most aware of? What emotions? Is your mind filled with churning thoughts? Take a moment to become aware of whatever is predominant, or the overall emotional tone of the situation.

A: *Allow Life to Be Just as It Is*

Send a message to your heart to "let be" this entire experience. Find in yourself the willingness to pause and accept that in these moments "what is . . . is." You can experiment with mentally whispering words like "yes," "I consent," or "let be."

You might find yourself saying yes to a huge inner "no," to a body and mind painfully contracted in resistance. You might be saying yes to the part of you that is saying, "I hate this!" That's a natural part of the process. At this point in RAIN, you are simply noticing what is true and intending not to judge, push away, or control anything you find.

I: *Investigate with a Gentle, Curious Attention*

Bring an interested and kind attention to your experience. Some of the following questions may be helpful. Feel free to experiment with them, varying the sequence and content.

- What is the worst part of this; what most wants my attention?
- What is the most difficult/painful thing I am believing?
- What emotions does this bring up (fear, anger, grief)?
- Where are my feelings about this strongest in my body? (Note: It's helpful to scan the throat, chest, and belly.)
- What are the feelings like (that is, the felt sense or sensations, such as clenched, raw, hot)?
- When I assume the facial expression and body posture that best reflect these feelings and emotions, what do I notice?
- Are these feelings familiar, something I've experienced earlier in my life?
- If the most vulnerable hurting part of me could communicate, what would it express (words, feelings, images)?
- How does this part want me to be with it?
- What does this part most need (from me or from some larger source of love and wisdom)?

A final note: Many students initially see "Investigate" as an invitation to fire up their cognitive skills—analyzing the situation or themselves, identifying the many possible roots of their suffering. This is a common misunderstanding, and it can distract from the essence of Investigation—awakening our somatic awareness. While mental exploration may enhance our understanding, opening to our embodied experience is the gateway to healing and freedom.

Instead of thinking about what's going on, keep bringing your attention to your body, directly contacting the felt sense and sensations of your most vulnerable place. Once you are fully present, listen for what this place truly needs to begin healing.

N: *Nurture with Loving Presence*

As you sense what is needed, what is your natural response? Calling on the most wise and compassionate part of your being, you might offer yourself a loving message or send a tender embrace inward. You might gently place your hand on your heart. You might visualize a young part of you surrounded in soft, luminous light. You might imagine someone you trust—a parent or pet, a teacher or spiritual figure—holding you with love. Feel free to experiment with ways of befriending your inner life—whether through words or touch, images or energy. Discover what best allows you to feel nurturing, what best allows the part of you that is most vulnerable to feel loved, seen, and/or safe. Spend as much time as you need, offering care inwardly and letting it be received.

After the RAIN

The four steps of RAIN involve active ways of directing our attention. *In After the RAIN, we shift from doing to being.* The invitation is to relax and let go into the heartspace that has emerged. Rest in this awareness and become familiar with it; this is your true home. Now, paying attention to the *quality* of your presence—the openness, wakefulness, tenderness—ask yourself:

- In these moments, what is the sense of my being, of who I am?
- How has this shifted from when I began the meditation?

Note: If you are still feeling raw, or a new difficulty comes up, include these feelings with kindness.

MEDITATION: CALLING ON YOUR FUTURE SELF

As you enter this meditation for future self, please feel free to substitute "wise self," "high self," "awakened heart," "awakened mind," or any other words that express your most evolved being.

—⊖—

Find a comfortable posture, close your eyes, and come into stillness. Take several long, deep breaths to collect your attention. See if with each out breath you can release any tension that has accumulated in your body.

Scan your current life, and let your attention go to a situation where you feel stuck in emotional reactivity—in fear, hurt, or anger.

Now gaze into the future ten or twenty years from now, and visualize your future self's home. Where in this home do you see your future self? Are you inside or outside? In a certain room? Are there pictures, furnishings, or plants nearby that hold a special meaning for you? How does your future self look—your clothing, your hair, your facial expression? What is the expression in your future self's eyes? Can you sense kindness? A caring welcome?

Take some moments to connect with the place where you feel most stuck and vulnerable, and then share your current difficulty with your future self.

Now imagine that your future self is offering healing attention and care to your current self. You might feel that you are receiving some touch of kindness, maybe an energetic embrace. You might receive a message of guidance, of reassurance. See how fully you can take in that warmth and care and wisdom. Feel your future self holding you and filling you with loving presence. Sense that whatever is most difficult right now—even the deepest fears and grief—can be included in this open and nurturing presence. Relax into your future self's embrace until you sense that you are fully merging with—at one with—your future self.

Take some moments to sense how the love and wisdom of your most evolved being lives in you now and always. Trust that with practice you can access this awakened, compassionate heartspace with more and more ease.

QUESTIONS AND RESPONSES

What if I can't get in touch with a future or high self?

Many people ask this because all of us, at times, feel cut off. When you're caught in emotional reactivity, the parts of you that hold generosity or kindness may seem worlds away, even nonexistent. It's not true; they are here! However, calling on the most evolved expression of your being is a life practice, and it becomes more powerful each time you reach out. Here are two approaches that can help you.

- Become alert to expressions of your awakening heart and mind as they appear in your daily life. You might be gazing at the night sky and fill with a sense of wonder. You might hug a friend who is hurting and feel very tender. You might be breathing mindfully and touch an inner stillness. You might hear someone you love judging themselves harshly and deeply wish they could see themselves through your eyes. Your awakened self is present at such times. Take a moment to *recognize and explore the felt sense of your experience.* This heartspace, this loving awareness, is your true nature. Become familiar with it. Perhaps whisper to yourself, "Remember this." Then, when you are stuck and reaching out, recall these moments. They will help you connect with the gold that is always and already here.

• When you feel stuck, act "as if" your future self were available, close by, listening, and aware of you. Even if it feels like going through the motions, mentally whisper your prayer or wish to know that caring presence in an intimate way. With practice, you'll discover that simply turning toward your future self brings you closer to that awake and kind presence.

How do I know if I'm deluding myself about my wise or future self?

Students often worry that they're just fantasizing, conjuring up whoever they wish they could be. This may be the case if your future self is a Nobel Prize winner, president, pope . . . or all three! But "future self" does not have to do with external accomplishments. Rather, it expresses who you are and how you live when your heart is open and your mind clear and awake.

You can imagine yourself in the future as wise and compassionate, because those capacities are already a part of you. Far from deluding yourself, you are actually calling forth your own potential when you reflect on your wise or future self. And the more you conjure up the qualities you most value, the more they become an ongoing, accessible part of your being.

What if RAIN's not working for me?

We've often spent decades living with persistent fears and emotional reactivity, and these painful tangles take time to unravel. It's quite natural to feel that what you're doing isn't working! There will be times when you try RAIN and end up feeling worse as you sense the potency of the old patterning. Or you might get stuck on any of the steps:

Recognize: You might feel agitated and confused, and when you try to pause and Recognize what's going on, you continue to feel swamped and unclear.

Allow: You might become aware of a deep sense of shame but not feel able to Allow it to be there.

Investigate: You might get in touch with irritation, Investigate, and have it explode into anger, get pulled into your angry stories, and instead of completing the practice, go back into your day carrying around that anger. Or you might Recognize anxiety, Allow it to be there for a few moments, start to Investigate, and then feel so anxious that you decide to go online and distract yourself.

Nurture: You might get in touch with self-judgment and self-hate and not find any way to Nurture the parts of your being that feel unlovable.

After the RAIN: You might think you've gone through the steps of RAIN, but then when you try to simply rest quietly in presence, you find you're restless, distracted, or anxious.

In any of these situations, you might conclude that RAIN didn't work. The truth is that any intentional movement toward presence, even when you relapse into trance, interrupts old patterning and serves your healing. Even if you get distracted, you can trust that you're experiencing the anxiety, shame, or anger with somewhat more presence. And trusting this will help you resume the practice when you are ready and continue the process of healing with RAIN.

As with all practices of healing and awakening, RAIN requires that you be patient, flexible, and willing to experiment.

- You may have a richer experience when you explore the steps of RAIN with a teacher or therapist or when you listen to a guided RAIN meditation. You might also find that RAIN comes alive when you do it with a friend. (See RAIN Partners, page 249.)
- You may benefit most when you've had a good night's sleep, or when you haven't just eaten (a lot of food, rich food, sweet food), or when you exercise or meditate before you practice with RAIN.
- You may need a certain setting that feels safe.
- You might find that a change in medication (adding, increasing, decreasing, eliminating) makes it easier to relate to your inner life.

If you put aside self-judgment, stay curious, and keep practicing, you'll find the approach to RAIN that best serves you on the path.

When I'm freaked out, I can't even remember my Social Security number. How am I supposed to remember the steps of RAIN?

It's true that the more entangled we get in emotional reactivity, the less we remember the way out. Many people find that the following reminders (which build on the first two questions, introduced in chapter 2) give them direct access to the steps:

- What is happening inside me? (*R*, Recognize)
- Can I be with this? (*A*, Allow)
- What is REALLY happening inside me? (*I*, Investigate)
- Can I be with this . . . with kindness? (*N*, Nurture)

Whenever you find yourself lost or confused, these questions can help you step back on the path.

PART II

Bringing RAIN to Your
Inner Life

FOUR

Releasing Negative
Self-Beliefs

We speak about losing our minds as if it is a bad thing.
I say, lose your mind. Do it purposefully. Find out who
you really are beyond your thoughts and beliefs.

• VIRONIKA TUGALEVA

One of the great blocks to realizing the gold of who we are is
our conviction that "something is wrong with me." When
I teach about the trance of unworthiness, I'm often asked,
"Why do we hold on so tightly to our belief in our own deficiency? Why are we so loyal to our suffering, so addicted to our
self-judgment?"

While we might long to accept and trust ourselves, trying
to release our negative self-beliefs can feel as if we were trying
to exorcise something buried deep inside our body. And in a
way we are.

Our beliefs live not only in our mind but in a constellation
of feelings and emotions embedded in our bodies. As a favorite
saying goes, "Our issues are in our tissues." They are deeply

familiar. They feel like "me." Most are rooted in interpretations of reality we formed in early childhood, and we rely on them for guidance and protection. They tell us who we are and what we can expect from ourselves, from others, and from the world.

Our most potent negative self-beliefs arise from early experiences of fear and wounding. Due to a survival-driven negativity bias, we remember painful events much more readily than pleasant ones. We remember the critical comment more than something affirming, the dog bite more than the beautiful sunset. As the psychologist Rick Hanson puts it, "The brain is Velcro for negative experiences, but Teflon for positive ones."

This fixation on what might be threatening is compounded by another tendency, called the confirmation bias, which leads us to focus on information that matches or reinforces our existing beliefs—particularly in the case of charged issues like our value as a person. The upshot: We make an airtight case for our belief in personal deficiency.

We keep the feelings of deficiency alive in daily life through our incessant inner dialogue. If you watch your thoughts, you may discover the Judge in the background, continually asking, "How am I doing?" and condemning the gap between some ideal standard and what is. You may also notice worry thoughts about how falling short is right around the corner, or how you'll be rejected for your flaws.

As long as we continue our fear-based thinking, our beliefs will maintain their potency. Writer Carlos Castaneda says that we maintain our world with our inner dialogue and that our world will change as soon as we stop talking to ourselves.

A traditional story from Polynesia captures the ultimate cost of obeying our fears and self-doubt.

In ancient times, a revered tribal leader went regularly to the river to shed her skin, each time returning to her village renewed and invigorated. But one day things changed. Instead of floating away, her old skin got caught in a bit of driftwood. And when she returned home, her daughter ran away from her in fear, because this raw-skinned new person no longer looked like her familiar self.

Finally, unable to comfort her daughter, the woman went back to the river, found her old skin, and put it back on. And from that time on, the story tells us, humans lost their power to rejuvenate, to live and love fully. They became mere mortals, entangled in fears of failure and the need to cover over their flaws.

AWAKENING FROM THE TRANCE OF UNWORTHINESS

The old skin that is most difficult to shed is our core belief that something is wrong with us—that we are deficient or flawed. In my work with meditation students and clients over the last decades, I've seen how this belief has stopped people from having intimate relationships, generated ongoing anxiety and depression, fueled addictive behavior, and caused harm to their loved ones. The philosopher Friedrich Nietzsche writes, "The snake that cannot shed its skin perishes." To flourish, we need to release the belief that something is wrong with us.

To examine the hook of negative self-beliefs, scan an arena in your life where you are down on yourself. Take a few moments to focus on what about the situation feels so bad. Now ask yourself:

What am I believing about myself? Is it that you're falling short? That you're bad for being hurtful to others? That you will be rejected? That you'll never get the intimacy or success you long for? That you are unlovable?

Now ask yourself this:

What is wrong with letting go of this belief? Or *What bad might happen if I let go of this self-judgment?* When I ask this question in workshops or with individuals, I hear answers like these:

"I'll never change and become who I want to be."

"I'm afraid I'd be even worse."

"I'd be powerless; there'd be no way to watch out for
   myself, protect myself."

"Others would judge me more, and I wouldn't be
   prepared for their criticism."

"I wouldn't know who I am."

"I wouldn't know how to live."

As we continue to investigate these beliefs together, some people also mention their fear of how others would react if they changed. Like the woman who went back to the river to soothe her daughter's upset, we keep our old skin to fit others' expectations. The experience of a flawed self can be comfortable in its familiarity. Often we build relationships with others around our shared insecurity. We develop dependent relationships from the role of the "deficient" or weak one. The youngest child in the family is always "the baby," the one who has struggled with drug abuse is "the addict," the domineering and aggressive one, "the alpha." Our self-identity is reinforced by what others believe about us, and we collude by staying the same. We'd rather protect the current relationship than risk rocking the boat.

Students often tell me that they need their self-judgments, that if they don't remember what's wrong with them, others will remind them. They tell me, "I'm not the only one who thinks I'm falling short; everyone else tells me that too." And for them, it feels dangerous to shed the protective skin of old beliefs; they don't want to be caught unawares.

So, our negative self-beliefs, even when deeply painful, often give us a sense of certainty, orientation, and control. We can easily stay entranced for years and decades, perpetuating our sense of unworthiness with a habitual narrative of self-judgment and fear-based thinking. It is only when we directly open ourselves to the suffering of this trance—how it cuts us off from others and from our own heart and spirit, how we don't *have* to believe we're flawed—that we begin to intuit the freedom possible in shedding old skin.

REAL BUT NOT TRUE

Janice, a single mom, was a friend who had started coming to my weekly meditation class. In addition to having a demanding job, she felt caught between the needs of Bruce, her fifteen-year-old son, who was struggling with social anxiety, and the needs of her dad, who lived for her visits. Twice a week, she'd leave work early and spend forty-five minutes navigating the evening rush hour to get to her dad's assisted-living facility. He always lit up when she arrived, and then, when she got up to leave, he'd anxiously ask when she was coming back. She resented him for making her feel guilty, resented the time away from work and her son, and, most deeply, resented herself for not being more openhearted and gracious.

Janice had begun to practice RAIN, but so far this tangle of resentment hadn't budged. Then, during one of our walks, she asked for my help. So I put on my meditation-teacher hat and asked her what she was believing about herself. She responded immediately, "I'm falling short on the most important fronts." Then, shaking her head with resignation, she went on: "You know, Tara, I'm failing them and . . . this is awful to say . . . but I'm just not a loving person."

When we hear such painful self-judgments from a friend, it's tempting to jump in with reassurance. "Of course you're a loving person. . . . Remember the time . . . ?" But instead I asked Janice something she didn't expect, a question the author Byron Katie uses in her work: "Is it true? Is it true that you're failing, and that you're not a loving person?"

She responded impatiently, "All the evidence points that way."

I asked again, "Are you certain that you're failing, that you're not a loving enough person? Is it really true?" This time she slowed down before replying.

"Okay, it really *feels* true, Tara. I'm not liking myself very much these days . . . but no . . . I guess I'm not certain." We walked in silence for a bit, and when I glanced at her, Janice looked thoughtful and sad but not so grim.

Then I shared a phrase I'd learned from one of my teachers:

"real but not true." Yes, our beliefs and the feelings under them are real; they exist in our body and mind and have tremendous power over us. But we need to ask ourselves this: Do they match the actual, living, changing stuff of our experience in the world? In other words, are they true?

Our thoughts are sound bites and/or images that form a map of reality in our mind. Some maps are useful. For instance, I may have a thought that if I drink too much caffeine, I won't be present with others. This can help guide my behavior. Other maps are harmful, for instance, the belief that if I say no to a friend, it proves that I'm a bad person.

In either case, we need to realize that these thoughts or beliefs are, as the Zen teachings say, like the finger pointing to the moon, not the moon itself.

In the following week's meditation class (without mentioning Janice), I came back to this idea. Our beliefs are real because we experience them mentally, emotionally, and physically. And they have real impact on our lives! As Gandhi put it, they lead to action, create our character, and shape our destiny. But these beliefs—even the ones that feel most true—are only mental representations or symbols of our experience.

It can be life changing to realize "I don't have to believe my thoughts . . . they are just thoughts!" Any story you have about yourself is not the same as the unfolding reality of what you are: the ongoing life of your senses, the tenderness of your heart, the consciousness that right now is seeing or hearing these words. Yet because our beliefs are continuously filtering and interpreting reality, we mistake our stories about ourselves and the world for reality itself. Understanding "real but not true" can free us from this prison.

In the weeks to come, these teachings created a tiny but important opening for Janice. She became more hopeful, more willing to deepen her attention. I've seen this over and over. When we have enough perspective to realize "I'm not my thoughts" or "This is just a belief," we are unhooking from the inner dialogue. This gives us choice. It enables us to wake up to a larger awareness.

RELEASING BELIEFS WITH RAIN

RAIN is a crucial help at this point, because it offers us a systematic way to loosen the grip of fear-based beliefs. Janice and I met again to go over the steps of RAIN together, and she began to practice daily, sometimes for only a few minutes, sometimes longer. Several weeks later, she shared an experience with me.

One afternoon, after she'd parked her car at her father's nursing home, she decided to do RAIN before going inside to visit. She reclined her seat, closed her eyes, and asked herself, "What is happening inside me?" A familiar voice in her head said, "This is the last thing I want to be doing right now. I just don't have the time." Her jaw was clenched. When she thought of her father, she felt dutiful, resentful, guilty, tight.

Janice was making the U-turn, turning her attention inward, and this was her starting place: She Recognized that cluster of feelings, and instead of judging herself for them, she simply Allowed herself to feel how painful they were without pushing them away. Then, after a few breaths, she leaned in, beginning to Investigate with interest, trying to get a better sense of what was going on. She gently asked herself, "What is the worst part about this?" and her attention went right to her chest. She felt heat, tightness, and pressure. "Ah," she said to herself, "I'm angry." And as she let the anger be there, it began to change shape. It morphed into a sense of powerlessness. There was no way she could live up to what was expected of her—with her father, with her son, at work. She was falling short; she would always fail. And now, along with that feeling of helplessness came self-condemnation: "I just don't like who I am. I don't like this grim, angry, closed-hearted, helpless self."

Investigating had connected her with what she had been running away from: the deep belief that she was failing and was an unloving person. She then recalled the question we had explored together: "Is it possible these beliefs are real but not true?" Asking this gave her enough space to stay present with what was unfolding.

She then asked, "When I'm believing this, what is my experience inside?" Her heart felt raw, tightly bound, and filled with a very childlike sense of helplessness and shame. She also felt an oppressive wave of fatigue. As she contacted this deep emotional pain in her body, she realized that these feelings had been buried within her for as long as she could remember. A natural response of sorrow and self-compassion arose.

Janice had reached the *N* of RAIN, Nurture, and with tears and with tenderness she began to whisper to herself, just as she would to a young child: "This is really difficult, and you're doing your best. You love Dad; you love Bruce. Now that you're here, you can relax. It's enough just to be with Dad now, love him now. It's okay."

She did relax, as if letting go into the arms of a wise, kind parent. She sat still for another five minutes or so, letting in and resting in the warmth and openness of this new space before she went inside. And when she peeked into her father's room, he was just waking from a nap.

He beamed at her and said, "I just had a dream about you as a little girl trying to ride Rosie." They laughed and began to share memories of Rosie, a much-loved dog, which led to more memories of good times. As she was leaving, Janice promised that for her next visit she'd bring some childhood pictures she had digitized. And when she got to her car, she realized that her father hadn't asked when she was coming back. She *was* back, and he wasn't so lonely.

RAIN had enabled Janice to reconnect with a very natural, openhearted sense of herself, but this didn't mean that her resentments, guilt, and negative beliefs magically disappeared. RAIN is rarely a one-shot experience; well-grooved beliefs and feelings continue to arise. The difference was, after weeks of practicing RAIN, Janice could see clearly that her beliefs weren't reality; they didn't have to confine her life experience and her sense of her own being.

Before Janice drifted off to sleep on the night of that visit, she reflected on how long she'd been hounded by a sense of her own deficiency. Then she asked herself one of the inquiries we'd discussed that can deepen the experience of After the RAIN: "Who would I be if I didn't believe this about myself?" The response was a spontaneous feeling of spaciousness, buoyancy, and warmth. Her spirit, she realized, was beyond any thought or belief. Trusting this gave Janice a true taste of peace.

WHO WE ARE BEYOND
OUR BELIEFS

While it may take numerous rounds, the four steps of RAIN can loosen the grip of even the most toxic, lifelong beliefs and reveal the freedom beyond a confining self-identity. If you pay attention to your experience during After the RAIN, you may discover the two fundamental flavors of this freedom:

- The first is what Buddhist psychology calls the realization of "no self" or emptiness. This refers to the lack of any confining sense of self-centeredness, self-solidity, or self-permanence. We are free from a limiting identity as a fearful or deficient or separate self.
- The second dimension of freedom is realizing the purity and fullness of awareness itself. We experience this boundless, wakeful, and tender presence as our very essence.

In the words of the Indian spiritual master Sri Nisargadatta, these radical expressions of freedom are inseparable:

> Wisdom tells me I'm nothing.
> Love tells me I am everything.
> And between the two my life flows.

During After the RAIN, a simple inquiry can help you experience your own awareness. Like Janice, you might ask, "Who am I if I no longer believe [limiting belief]?" Or alternately, "Who am I if nothing is wrong with me?" Even a glimpse of "no self" and/or oneness is a taste of the gold.

JUDGING OURSELVES, JUDGING OTHERS

Bruce was changing along with his mom. For several years, Janice had been worried that her son's anxiety kept him from finding friends and doing well in school. But as she began to relax her sense of personal failure, she started relaxing about Bruce too. Now, at dinnertime, she found herself enjoying his wry humor and quick observations, and listening from her office later in the evenings, she was impressed with his guitar playing. She became more confident he'd find his way, and something rubbed off. He began playing music with two boys in his class and seemed more at ease with himself.

One day during spring break, he asked to go with her to visit Granddad and play him a few songs on his new guitar. This was a major shift; he'd always refused. From then on, until her dad's death a year later, they'd go together every few weeks—a ritual of strumming, singing, and chatting enjoyed by all three. Releasing the grip of her own beliefs directly increased the well-being of the dear ones in Janice's life.

When we're convinced we're selfish, we're inclined to suspect the same of others. If we hate ourselves for being needy, we may feel repelled or frightened by neediness in others. And if we feel we're failing, we may look for signs of failure in those we're close to. Our negative self-beliefs become a powerful lens that shapes our experience of others; we can't see who's really there.

Stepping out of our old skin gives us a fresh and clear view. Not only are we able to sense the sincerity and benevolence of our own heart and being, but we are more able to see the gold shining through others. This growing trust in basic goodness is one of the gifts of the practice of RAIN.

TAKING "THE EXQUISITE RISK"

At this point you may be thinking, "Yes, I'd love to drop my judgments and feelings of failure . . . but they're so persistent!"

True, and it's important to respect how deeply rooted that sense of "something is wrong with me" can be. I used to despair of just how deep! It helped when I began to think in evolutionary terms. The fear of falling short is rooted in our survival brain, which has been shaping our existence for millions of years. This ancient fear keeps us holding on to the defensive skin of negative beliefs. Yet there's also a powerful urge toward our full potential—an urge to emerge as a more integrated, intelligent, compassionate being.

Because RAIN offers an attentive care to the fears arising from our survival brain, it brings us above the line, enabling us to heed the call of our future self. Yet these conflicting pulls continue to create a very natural tension in each of us.

When we shed our old skin, when we loosen the protective covering of our convictions, when we step free from our negative beliefs about ourselves and others, we are taking what the poet Mark Nepo calls "the exquisite risk." It's a risk because, as with all growth, we are exposing ourselves to the unknown, to danger, and to loss. It's exquisite because the natural beauty, sensitivity, and responsiveness of our being are awakened and revealed.

All individual and collective transformation requires willingly engaging with this risk. Our negative self-beliefs can keep us constricted, small-minded, disconnected from our heart, and suffering. Or we can take them as a call to Investigate, a call to take the exquisite risk with the mindfulness and radical compassion of RAIN. When we do, we begin to discover who we are beyond any thoughts or beliefs. And we begin to manifest our unlimited capacity for openhearted awareness.

MEDITATION: UPROOTING PAINFUL BELIEFS WITH RAIN

The Investigation step in this version of the RAIN meditation is particularly geared to unpack and loosen the grip of beliefs that cause suffering.

$\ominus$

Sitting comfortably, collect your attention with a few long, deep breaths. Take some moments to scan your body and relax any obvious areas of tension.

Bring to mind a belief that causes suffering in your life. Or if you are suffering right now, ask yourself, "What am I believing?" Is it something about yourself—that you're undeserving, a failure, too damaged to ever be happy or loved, always falling short? Do you hear someone else's voice—"weird," "loser," "you can never trust anybody"?

To connect fully with this belief, you might remind yourself of a particular situation that brought it up—or one that is likely to. Visualize the situation as clearly as possible. What do you see around you? Who else is there? What were you thinking and feeling?

Recognize: Your thoughts and feelings express a belief. What are you believing right now?

Allow: Pause for a few moments, and simply let the belief and accompanying feelings be there.

Investigate: Begin by asking, "Is this really true?" or "Am I certain this is true?"

Then ask, "What is it like to live with this belief?" You can deepen your Investigation by making the U-turn, turning from your thoughts to bring your attention to your body. What feelings and sensations are strong? Are particular emotions associated with this belief? Do you sense fear or shame, anger or self-hatred?

Widen the investigation by asking, "How has living with this belief affected my life?" Can you see its impact on how you relate to yourself and others, on your creativity, your capacity to serve, your ability to enjoy experience, your inner growth?

At this point, you might pause and ask yourself, "What is it like to honestly see and feel how this belief has shaped my life?"

Now turn your attention back to your body. Investigate the hurts and fears that live under the belief and drive it. And connecting with whatever feels most vulnerable right now, ask, "What do you most need?"

Nurture: Now bring your wisest and most loving self—your future self, your awake heart—to witness and feel your vulnerability. What message, touch, energy, or image might bring the most healing to the wounds inside you? Offer that, and let the place of vulnerability receive and be bathed in that nurturing energy.

After the RAIN: Notice the quality of presence that has unfolded, and rest in this space of awareness. After some moments, ask yourself, "What would my life be like without this belief?" and/or "Who would I become if I no longer lived with this belief?"

Whatever arises, rest in that experience. Let it fill you and get familiar with it.

QUESTIONS AND RESPONSES

What if this belief has proven true in my life again and again?

The nature of strong beliefs is that they directly influence our feelings and behaviors and consequently the way our life unfolds. For example, if you are insecure about being desirable or lovable, you're likely either to grasp onto potential partners out of your need for connection or to hide your vulnerability out of your fear of rejection. The belief sets you up for another failed relationship and traps you in a repeating loop of belief-action-failure-belief.

You might ask yourself, "Do I know for sure that I'll always be rejected?" Do you? No matter what our past experience, the nature of neuroplasticity is that we have potential for change. When you loosen the grip of your belief, you make room for an alternate future.

This holds true in our beliefs about the outside world. You might believe that you could never feel close to someone who has a different political ideology, or team up and work together toward a shared goal. But do we really know this for sure? If we challenge this kind of belief, we open ourselves to the dialogues between parties, races, genders, and religions that are necessary to awaken compassion and heal our world.

In your personal life, even a bit of openness about the future will allow you to bring more curiosity and gentleness to the present. You will be able to contact the wounds that give rise to the belief. Attending to this vulnerability will allow you to heal the roots of the belief, and you will begin to navigate your relationships with more confidence, flexibility, and freedom.

I see my negative side pretty clearly. If I dismiss my faults as "beliefs," won't I just indulge them even more?

Every one of us has parts of our character or ego covering that we would like to change. We act in ways we call selfish, aggressive, addictive, insensitive, neglectful—and on and on. And yes, depending on the severity of our unmet needs, these actions may cause harm to ourselves and others. We need to recognize how these behaviors bring suffering and create distance in our lives with others.

But there's a world of difference between the wisdom of discernment and the aversion of judgment. Discernment tells us, "When I insist on having things my way, my partner withdraws and becomes cold and distant." Judgment says, "Wanting things my own way means I'm selfish—a bad person." Judgment brands our fundamental being.

Recall the Golden Buddha in chapter 3. What's important is realizing the difference between the covering and the gold. You may act in selfish ways, but you are not intrinsically selfish. You are a being like most of us—spirit, awareness, love—with conditioned layers of selfishness. Identifying with the coverings ("I am a selfish person") only reinforces your self-beliefs and obscures the gold.

When you bring RAIN directly to the experience of any fault or flaw, you'll discover the vulnerability that drives it, and you'll awaken your capacity for self-compassion. This will naturally loosen the grip of selfishness or any other covering that limits you. You will be able to shed that old skin and renew your life.

FIVE

Freeing Yourself
from Shame

You, Beloved, put your lips on my forehead . . . and
lit a Holy Lamp inside my heart.

• HAFIZ, "KEEPING WATCH"

In almost every spiritual and religious tradition, the word "home" refers to the sacred space where we experience connection or belonging. Chronic shame severs that life-giving belonging. It covers over the gold of our spirit and sends us into exile, from ourselves and from others.

Not all shame is toxic. Shame wants us to survive, which for early humans meant having a group to protect them. The basic message from our survival brain is "I've done something wrong. If people find out, they'll send me away." Shame arises when our behavior has veered from societal norms, and with shame comes fear—the fear of being seen and banished. When shame is healthy, it spurs us to change our behavior in a positive way or to make amends so that we are part of the group again, and our shame recedes.

But shame turns toxic when it says, "There's something

wrong with me. I can't belong as I am." Then it's no longer a passing emotion, and we become identified as a "bad" or "deficient" self. We are easily taken over by negative self-beliefs, and we may become so sunk in self-aversion that offering kindness and care to ourselves feels impossible.

That is why this chapter will focus on the Nurture step of RAIN and on the many creative ways practitioners have found to access it. I'll enter this terrain through one of the best-known shame stories from the Bible, a Rembrandt painting, and the spiritual awakening of a contemporary Catholic priest.

THE PRODIGAL SON: LEAVING AND RETURNING HOME

A prosperous man has two sons, and the younger goes to his father and asks to have his portion of their inheritance early. When his father agrees, he leaves home, goes into another country, and squanders his inheritance in "riotous living." Then a famine comes, and he is reduced to herding pigs and eating their feed. Destitute and starving, he realizes that even his father's servants have more to eat, and he decides to return home and call on the mercy of his father.

Much to his relief, his father receives him with forgiveness, love, and great celebration for his homecoming. Seeing this, the older brother confronts his father with anger and jealousy. He had been obedient through the years. Why was he not the focus of this joyful celebration? The father proclaims his unconditional love—"My son, you are with me always and all I have is yours. But it was only right that we should celebrate and rejoice, because your brother here was dead and has come to life; he was lost and is found."

Rembrandt's famous painting shows the prodigal son, filthy and in tatters, kneeling before his father, his head bowed in shame. The old man bends over to bless him, his powerful left hand on his son's shoulder, holding him as if to say, "I see you and you belong. I see who you are." His right hand rests gently on his son's back, caressing, nourishing, maternal. He is the embodiment of wisdom and compassion, the sacred masculine and the sacred feminine. And there, off to one side, standing in shadow, is the older brother, rigid with resentment and judgment.

EMBRACING THE DIFFERENT FACES OF SHAME

Three centuries later this painting changed the course of spiritual life for the Dutch Catholic priest and author Henri Nouwen. As he recounts in his book *The Return of the Prodigal Son*, his first realization was how fully he identified with the younger brother's shame. He too had left his family home and sought to fill an inner vacuum by grasping at things outside himself—approval, success, renown. But as he reflected deeply on the painting, he experienced a further insight: He was also the older brother, the one whose judgment and blame had blocked him from feeling spiritually at home. His deep self-aversion and his anger, envy, and resentment of others had kept him from receiving the nurturing embrace from the father—a larger source of loving.

Finally, the pain and longing aroused in honestly facing these parts of himself shifted something: Nouwen surrendered his armor and became receptive to the father's forgiveness, compassion, and love. And in letting in that love, he began awakening beyond the constricting identity of a flawed, separate self. He wrote:

> Then both sons in me can gradually be transformed into the compassionate father. This transformation leads me to the fulfillment of the deepest desire of my restless heart. Because what greater joy can there be for me than to stretch out my tired arms and let my hands rest in a blessing on the shoulders of my home-coming children?

LETTING IN LOVE

I've had many encounters with the grasping of the younger brother and the aversive shaming of the elder. While my self-compassion has grown, there have been times of feeling entirely cut off from my heart. One of these times stands out because it opened a pathway to feeling nurtured—letting in love—that has been central to my practice ever since.

One winter about eight years ago, after a dense stretch of teaching and family visiting for the holidays, I entered the silence of a two-week retreat. Within twenty-four hours, I was swamped by guilt and regret. How come I didn't get around to having that talk with my brother? Why had I sniped at my sister over the timing of our get-togethers? Was I really present at that solstice event? I kept seeing more ways I was inattentive, preoccupied, and selfish. Here I was again, in a state I knew all too well—mucking around in the trance of unworthiness.

"Okay," I told myself, "it's time for RAIN." After I Recognized and Allowed my feelings of guilt, I started Investigation by naming the belief behind those feelings: "I should be a better, more loving, generous person." Then, as my attention dropped into my body, I contacted a familiar sinking feeling and a hollow, achy darkness in my chest and belly.

Then I tried to offer myself Nurture with a touch on my heart and some words of care, but some angry part of me dug in its heels. "But it's really not okay. I'm not okay. I'm selfish and unloving, and I don't want to be this way!"

Then the anger turned to helplessness and I began crying. I was hating how I was and afraid I'd never change. Now a deeper core belief emerged: "I am unlovable."

When I asked what this deep place of feeling unlovable most needed, I suddenly found myself whispering out loud, "Please love me." Over and over, the plea, "Please love me."

And then I became aware of a very intimate presence— a field of sentience and light that surrounded me, a presence that was entirely tender and compassionate. I bowed my head slightly and sensed a kiss on my brow—a blessing of pure acceptance and care. Something in me opened, and I was bathed in loving light.

The more light I let in, the more any sense of separation fell away. Whatever arose—sounds of the wind outside, a tingling in my body, a memory of a friend who'd died, a wave of sorrow at how self-judging persists—all was held in this luminous, open heartspace. I heard the whispered words of an Indian teacher, "Love is always loving you," and knew them to be true.

Since that experience, at times of difficulty, I've often called on that intimate presence. I sense the blessing at my brow and then feel myself held in compassion. But I've also learned not to wait for difficulty. Now there are many moments—between emails, in the shower, before giving a talk—when I pause, turn toward presence, let in love, and become that field of loving.

With daily repetition, this pathway to Nurturing has become ever more alive, intimate, and familiar. The more I bathe in the experience of loving and being loved, the more accessible it becomes in daily life. Yes, the old patterns—the selfishness, self-judgments, and fears—keep arising, but they are now held in a heartspace that is all-inclusive and tender.

REACHING OUT FOR LOVE AND BELONGING

The core feeling of shame is a sense of personal badness, and with shame comes self-aversion, fear, and the urge to hide. We are isolated, no longer a part of the circle of life. The medicine for shame is radical compassion, the loving presence that helps us trust our belonging and essential goodness.

That afternoon when I called out, "Please love me," I didn't have a name for what I was doing. I now understand it as a way of accessing our inner sources of Nurturing—of loving and feeling loved—that are not available through the "doings" of the small self.

When we're infants, we depend on those around us as sources of love and care. And as developmental psychologists have shown, we humans have the inborn capacity to internalize that loving with remarkable speed. If all goes well, we build inner resources of love, safety, happiness, belonging, and strength that we can draw on throughout life.

But here we're exploring another crucial fact: Even if those positive inner states were not created early, or even if emotions like shame have cut us off from them, we can still find ways to Nurture and develop those resources. *At any time in our lives, we can cultivate our access to the inner experience of love and belonging.* Through the Nurture step of RAIN, we can learn to trust our essential goodness.

RESOURCE ANCHORS: ACCESS TO SOURCES OF NURTURING

When we can't access self-compassion, it's time to find other sources of Nurture. We look outside ourselves for living experiences and exemplars of kindness that have particular meaning for us and then call on them to nourish our hearts. I call these resource anchors because they build and stabilize the inner resources we are developing.

Here are some resource anchors that students have shared with me:

- I visualize sitting with my grandmother at her kitchen table, put my hand on my heart, and imagine her kindness is pouring in.
- I carry around a photo of my son when he was two years old, sleeping with his head on our old golden retriever. When I'm stuck, I look at it and feel the loving I've forgotten.

- I visualize the Dalai Lama, imagine he's looking right at me, caring about me, including me in his heart.
- I curl up with my dog, or if she isn't around, imagine how excited she is every time I get home, how she sleeps pressed against my legs.
- I say 'Please love me' and imagine the trees and birds, the flowers, rocks, and all creatures are sending me love.
- I imagine my future self—totally fearless, welcoming, warm, compassionate—and ask him for help.
- I call on Kwan Yin, the bodhisattva of compassion, and visualize a radiance surrounding me and imagine it entering and filling me with her mercy and kindness.
- I ask my partner to hold me, and if she isn't there, imagine her arms around me.
- I wear a bracelet—a beaded lapis mala—and when I take it off and feel each bead carefully, there's a link to Buddha nature, to compassion, to presence.
- I softly recite a short Jewish prayer my grandfather taught me, and it reminds me of his loving heart, and of the love in the universe.
- I lie down on the earth, or lean against a large old oak tree behind our home. I let my sorrows be held by the vastness of the earth and sky. And if I'm in my windowless cubicle twelve stories up, I imagine all of that.
- I put my hand on my heart and repeat phrases of loving kindness for myself and others—May I be happy, free from danger, at peace. May you be happy, free from danger, at peace.

- I remember other people I know who are suffering as I am, feel us as a community of beings, the shared humanness of it.

CUSTOMIZING YOUR PATH OF NURTURING

In the chapters to come, I'll offer other approaches to building our resources, many of them based on experiences shared by my students. Here are two examples of how relationships with a seemingly outside source brought deep healing to shame.

A young woman, Brenda, relapsed after five years in recovery from alcoholism. She regained her sobriety, but months later, and even with the support of her AA group, she was consumed by shame and self-hatred. Whenever she made any attempt to access self-compassion, she hit a wall of anger and despair.

Then Brenda learned "Calling on Your Future Self," the meditation taught in chapter 3. She began to build a picture of herself as a forgiving, wise, and vibrant middle-aged woman, standing with her two dogs in a beautiful field. This image became a resource anchor and a part of her daily practice: She'd imagine her future self's clear blue eyes and welcoming smile and feel a sense of inner comfort and ease. Then, after some weeks, she intentionally brought her sense of shame and failure to her future self and asked for help. In response, she heard a whisper: "You are more than this addiction . . . trust your caring heart." Warmth and light filled her, and she felt that her future self was already with her, inside her.

Brenda's shame and harshness toward herself didn't just vanish. But after six months of practice she told me, "Having my future self inside me feels more like the truth of who I am than any of the negative stories I still tell myself."

Sean had lost his job during the 2008 recession, and after sixteen months of looking and dozens of rejections, he spiraled into depression. When he came to one of my weekly meditation classes, he was honest about the deep shame he was feeling and about how he was isolating himself. He'd tried RAIN, but the Nurture step stumped him. "I feel like a loser, and I can't dig up an iota of self-compassion," he told me.

When I asked Sean if anyone related to him with care or understanding, he mentioned his wife, who had been consistently kind. But he couldn't accept her reassurances, because, as he put it, "I'm supposed to support my family. I'm not holding up my end." Then, after a long pause, he mentioned his long-standing men's group. I suggested that in addition to their in-person support he could make the group a resource anchor, one that he could access at any time. "Try to visualize the faces of the guys who really get how tough it is," I suggested, "and then let their care and concern sink in." Sean became very quiet.

After a while, I asked him what he was feeling. "It's hard to put into words," he said, "but they make me feel like they respect me, job or no job. That I matter just as a human being." And then he choked up a bit: "We're in it together . . . connected. It warms me up; I feel more alive."

I urged Sean to pay attention to that warm sense of connection and to let it really fill his body. He was accessing the healing of Nurturing, and now, during After the RAIN, he could let this healing deepen. "Sense what is important to you about these feelings, and try to memorize them," I said. "The more often you think of your friends and bring these feelings alive inside you, the more your inner resources will be there for you when you need them."

CALLING ON THE EARTH GODDESS

Reaching toward a larger source of loving is a natural and powerful pathway of Nurturing our inner resources, one that has been used by countless beings, including the Buddha-to-be.

In chapter 2, I shared the broad strokes of the Buddha's enlightenment, how Siddhartha spent the entire night meditating under the Bodhi tree, even as the god Mara sent his demons to shake his resolve. Now I'll add a key piece that was essential to his, and is to our, freedom: While Siddhartha met the demons with compassion and mindfulness, he was not yet completely liberated. As night began to fade, Mara issued his greatest challenge: By what right did Siddhartha aspire to Buddhahood? In other words, "Who do you think you are?" And Mara demanded that Siddhartha produce a witness to confirm his awakening.

Then Siddhartha reached out his right hand and touched the earth. And the earth goddess rose up, responding with a roar: "I am your witness." The earth shook, and Mara vanished. And as dawn broke, Siddhartha became the Buddha.

Even the Buddha-to-be faced doubt and challenges to his worth. By calling on a larger presence, he realized and affirmed his true belonging to all of life and freed his heart from doubt. We too can learn to touch the ground and call on an outer source of Nurturing. We too can cultivate the inner resources of love and belonging that heal the pain of shame.

MEDITATION: LETTING IN LOVE

Sitting comfortably with your eyes closed, take a few moments to breathe, feel into your body, and relax obvious areas of tension.

Bring to mind a situation where you are filled with self-judgment or self-aversion and unable to hold yourself with compassion. Visualize what's going on, and remind yourself of the worst part of this situation, what really makes you feel that "something is wrong with me."

Allow yourself to contact the vulnerable place in your body that feels that you are bad, unlovable, or unworthy. Try to open to the felt sense of shame by paying particular attention to your throat, heart, and belly. You might find that breathing in and out of that vulnerable place helps to sustain your attention.

From this inner place, imagine the kind of Nurture that would feel most comforting, most healing. Would it be words that affirm your goodness and worth? A hug? A tender and accepting presence?

Now sense who you most wish would be the source of that Nurture. Whose love would feel most healing? Whose care would you most trust? You might imagine a dear friend, a child, a dog, a tree, a grandparent—even one who's no longer alive. You might bring to mind a teacher or a spiritual figure, such as the Buddha, Kwan Yin, the Great Mother, Jesus. You might experience a formless presence of your own high self, your future or realized being.

Feel how much you long to be truly seen, loved, held. Then, either silently or in a whisper, call on the source of loving you have chosen. You might say, "Please love me," "Please hold me," or "Please take care of me," and repeat softly whatever words most fully express your longing.

Imagine being heard. Imagine that your vulnerability and longing are felt by that presence. If the being has eyes, imagine them looking at you, receiving you, with total love, understanding, and care.

Sense their love as an energetic presence that surrounds you and soaks into you. Be like an absorbent sponge, letting it in. You might feel the love filling your body like a warm glow, or visualize it as a flow of golden nectar, penetrating into the hollows and crevices, soothing and healing the most wounded places inside you.

Allow yourself to bathe in this loving . . . to surrender and let go into the loving more and more fully . . . to dissolve into oneness with that loving presence. Become the tender field that your small self is floating in, the loving awareness that is holding your life. As you get to know this heartspace, it will increasingly feel like home.

Before ending the meditation, take some moments to listen. Is there a message from this heartspace, something to remember, that feels important?

QUESTIONS AND RESPONSES

When I'm stuck in shame, how can I find self-compassion? I get to the Nurture step, but I feel unworthy of any care. Going through the motions just highlights how bad I feel about myself.

What you describe makes sense: When we're at war with ourselves, our entire mind-set and our biochemistry are at odds with self-compassion. So how do we begin to shift? Our hearts start to soften as we deepen our attention to the suffering within us. Instead, all too often, we judge our feelings, thinking, "I shouldn't be feeling this shame, this anger at myself, this fear of what others think." We also compare our situation with those of others and tell ourselves, "They have it worse." And so we decide we don't deserve kindness.

It helps to "start where you are," which means starting RAIN fresh. Recognize and Allow how bad you feel about yourself, and then Investigate. Notice what it feels like in your body to be so caught in shame, the unpleasantness of that. You might sense how long you've lived this way—believing something's wrong with you, that you don't deserve care—and how that has kept you from living fully. Take some time to connect with the suffering of shame—how it affects your body, heart, and mind. The moment you can honestly say, "Oh, this is painful . . . I'm hurting," you will sense a natural arising of sorrow and self-compassion.

What if I can't find any larger source of loving affirmation?

When we feel cut off and ashamed, many of us find it hard to trust that there is any loving available anywhere. This is especially so if we had little nurturing in our early years or, worse, were neglected or abused. While it may take longer to develop a reliable pathway of resourcing, the good news is that it's possible. I've seen thousands of people from diverse upbringings, and with much emotional suffering, find their way to a source of loving.

The trick to resourcing love is to look for what I call a tendril of loving. Perhaps there's a relationship where you don't feel the full warmth of love, but you sense there's a potential for care that you'd like to experience. When you practice the above meditation, "Letting in Love," be creative. Look wherever in this living world you feel even a small sense of resonance.

With practice, you can strengthen that tendril of loving so that it becomes a vital pathway of connection.

After you've found even a tendril of loving, pause and let it soak in and fill you. Feel it in your body as warmth, light, aliveness . . . however it expresses itself. Take at least fifteen to thirty seconds to get familiar with it.

And finally, repeat this process regularly. Your tendril will develop shoots and in time flower with the full fragrance of love.

***Others are giving me the message that something's
really wrong with me. How do I know they're
not right?***

There's an important distinction between messages
that let us know how we're impacting others (and perhaps
ourselves) and messages that say, "This makes you a bad
person." For example, it may be uncomfortable to hear
something like "Your judgments and anger make me feel
unsafe," but it's potentially useful information. We grow
by being open to feedback. But any message that implies
we're basically flawed is untrue.

Commit yourself to not believing messages of
badness. If a message brings up shame, recall the
discussion of "real but not true" in chapter 4. The feelings
of shame may be all too real, but they do not express the
truth about you. Meet your inner experience with
self-compassion, or bring to mind someone who loves
you and sense that they are holding you with kindness.
Remember your basic goodness, and let your deepest
intention be to trust your awakening heart and mind.

We're in this together: The most insidious messages of
badness are those embedded in our society. Cultures are
organized around stories of good/bad, right/wrong,
superior/inferior, and they invoke shame to varying
degrees in all of us. These stories target the way we treat
each other, how much we earn, what we consume, the
shape of our body, how we express creativity, our spiritual
or religious beliefs, our gender, the color of our skin.
Social shame served human evolution by enforcing
cohesiveness in early tribes, and it can still alert us to

behavior that threatens our belonging. But it has a very big shadow. Society's messages—about the proper role and behavior of women, about the inferior status of people of color, about the unnaturalness of nonheterosexual orientations, and more—continue to cause horrific shame, oppression, injustice, and suffering. We'll explore this more in part 3, but please keep in mind that embedded in the message "something is wrong with you," there is often a societal story that is invisible, shaming, and toxic.

SIX

Awakening from the Grip of Fear

We are not the survival of the fittest, we are the survival of the nurtured.

• LOUIS COZOLINO

In a distant land, word spread far and wide of a holy man with magic so powerful it could relieve the most severe suffering. But to reach his wilderness refuge and receive his healing, a seeker had to trek through dense forests and over precarious mountain passes. Those who persevered arrived at the holy man's simple hut exhausted and dirty. After guiding them to a refreshing stream and then offering tea, he'd sit with them in silence, gazing out at the pines and sky. When he finally spoke, it was to swear them to secrecy about what was next to pass between them. Once they took the vow, the holy man asked a single question: "What are you unwilling to feel?"

THE SUFFERING OF RESISTING FEAR

If you're feeling trapped in emotional pain, the holy man's question may seem confusing or even offensive. But if you look again, you might discover the resistance surrounding the pain, a fear of actually feeling your fear that keeps suffering locked in place.

Especially when fear is intense, we're afraid we'll drown in it, be annihilated. So, to varying degrees, our primitive survival brain prompts us to cut off the raw emotional energy in our body; we bury or numb our feelings and preoccupy ourselves with thoughts. But when we pull away from fear and other painful emotions, we also pull away from our full presence and vitality. We pull away from our intelligence, creativity, and capacity for love.

Sometimes our unwillingness to experience our feelings shows up as depression. Sometimes it takes the form of chronic anxiety or irritation, with our muscles and posture tightening into what I often call "Worrier Pose." It can appear as loneliness, restlessness, boredom, or a sense of operating on autopilot. And it often manifests as addictive behavior.

Whatever the expression, resisting fear puts us in a trance.

Remember the circle of awareness in chapter 1? Everything above the line is in awareness, and everything below the line is not. When we resist fear, we are living partially below the line—identified with the fear, and cut off from our full lucidity and presence. Our unfelt, unprocessed fear is operating outside awareness to shape our beliefs, decisions, and actions. The fear we are unwilling to feel controls and binds our life.

A friend told me this story. When her son was six, he had a recurring nightmare of being chased by a monster. It was very big and dark, and no matter how fast he ran, the monster was always right behind him. The dream was so terrifying and appeared so frequently that he was afraid to go to sleep. One night at bedtime, his mom held his hand and said, "You know, if that monster turns up tonight, here's something to try. Instead of running, turn around and see what it looks like so you can tell me. Okay?" Early the next morning her son ran excitedly into her bedroom. He had faced the monster and . . . it wasn't real! It was just an oversized bad guy from a favorite video game, and when he looked it right in the face, it dissolved.

You might say, "It's fine to face down an imagined monster and watch it dissolve. But what about real dangers?" Whether or not there's an actual risk, facing and opening to the emotional experience of fear allows us to come above the line and access our natural resourcefulness. It calls forth our reason and clarity, courage and compassion. Running away only amplifies the felt sense of being powerless and afraid.

Because our ways of avoiding fear are both habitual and largely unconscious, turning to face fear requires intention and presence. RAIN can help us make the U-turn: Recognizing and Allowing fear to be there, and then deepening our presence in a way that reduces fear's power. With practice, we discover that when our resistance is gone, the demons are gone. We may still feel fear, but we are above the line, reconnected to a larger space of presence and self-compassion.

AWAKENING FROM THE GRIP OF FEAR

TURNING TOWARD FEAR WITH RAIN

After a daylong seminar on RAIN and stress, Brianna came up to me and asked for some help with a personal situation. She'd recently been hired as a marketing vice president in a large corporation, but she felt intimidated by the CEO, who was very quick to cut off anyone who was "wasting his time." He ruled over the weekly staff meetings, which Brianna described as "torture" that put her into a state of "brain freeze." "I shouldn't be worried about my competence," she said. "I was recruited because I got an industry award at my last job. But the atmosphere here is totally different—really corporate, and the other VPs pretty much ignore me. I just go back to my office with my stomach churning and wonder how long I'll last. Do you think RAIN can help me?"

I suggested that Brianna practice RAIN for a few minutes right before each meeting and asked her what was going on for her at that time.

"On those mornings, I can really feel the anxiety building, and it lands me in a frenzy of busyness . . . reviewing reports, marking what I might need to comment on . . . nothing really productive."

I smiled because I recognized that feeling all too well. "Okay, so before you start RAIN, imagine you're pressing the pause button on that frenzy."

Brianna closed her eyes and pictured herself at her desk, half an hour before the weekly meeting. "As you pause," I said, "your first job is to Recognize the anxiety and Allow it to be there." After she nodded, I added, "Now, what do you notice if you bring your attention and interest to how it feels in your body?"

Beginning to Investigate, she muttered, "Dry mouth . . . really tight chest . . . heart hammering . . . and, oh yeah, my stomach's in knots." I suggested she place her hand on her abdomen and send her breath there with a long, slow inflow and outflow. This would help her steady her attention and stay in contact with the fear.

Now I guided her to ask the scared place inside her what it needed most. After a moment, she looked up, surprised. "The fear needs to feel accepted . . . that it belongs and it's okay that it's here."

So the Nurturing that scared place needed was to be accepted, not to be made "wrong." I asked Brianna how the wisest, kindest part of her wanted to respond. Could she find a way to acknowledge this very vulnerable part of herself? She sat quietly, still breathing slowly, her hand on her belly. Then she nodded. "I just sent the message 'It's okay . . . this belongs.' And . . . it does feel more okay. I'm actually a bit more relaxed."

Brianna's message was truly healing and wise. Like an ocean, we have many waves of different feelings, and they all belong; they are part of us. When we encounter the difficult ones like hurt or fear and acknowledge "this belongs," there's a natural sense of enlarging and more ease with what is moving through us.

This became Brianna's RAIN practice each week before going to the staff meeting: After pressing the pause button, she'd Recognize and Allow the fear, Investigate as she breathed with it, put her hand where the feelings were most intense, and offer a comforting "It's okay. This belongs." When she felt anxiety spike during the meeting, she'd simply breathe into it and send that same message.

About three months later, Brianna updated me. Her tension around the CEO hadn't disappeared, but her anxiety had lessened somewhat. More important, it didn't feel like such a big deal: "It's not so alarming when I get anxious. . . . I'm not taking it so personally," she told me. "I was fighting it so hard, but now it's okay that it's there. Accepting it seems to loosen the brain freeze. It really does free me up."

Brianna was experiencing the fruits of RAIN in her work life. When we're stuck and reactive, anxiety feels totally personal—a negative commentary about ourselves. RAIN loosens that identification, so that instead of an emotion that defines and possesses us, anxiety becomes more like a familiar inner weather system—unpleasant, but not a problem.

Brianna told me she'd made an appointment with the CEO to propose a risky but creative marketing strategy and that she'd won his backing. She'd also made a friendly alliance with a colleague down the hall and was getting to know a couple of others. "And you know," she said, "there's some real excitement mixed in with the anxiety now. I'm on my edge and growing."

When anxiety arises, we are conditioned to assume that something is wrong and that we need to act to protect ourselves. Yet, as Mark Twain put it, "the worst things in my life never actually happened." With practice, we catch on to this habit of anticipating trouble, of looking for something to worry about. Then we can say to ourselves, "It's just anxiety, it's okay . . . this belongs," and begin to unhook from a lifetime pattern of reactivity.

WHEN FEAR FEELS LIKE "TOO MUCH"

Although Brianna's anxiety was disabling at work, she still had enough presence and focus to practice RAIN. But when fear becomes acute and we feel panicked or powerless, we become unable to access presence. At these times, attempting to turn toward and Investigate our experience has the potential to re-traumatize us or reinforce the fear. We are pushed outside our "window of tolerance."

This phrase was coined by the psychiatrist and author Daniel Siegel, and it's a useful tool for anyone struggling with fear, rage, or other strong emotions. Each person's window of tolerance is different. You've surely noticed how your resilience varies from day to day—and also over longer periods, shrinking when you're under prolonged stress, expanding when things are going well. The good news is that whatever your circumstances, you can expand your window of tolerance (or what psychologists call your degree of affect tolerance) by doing the inner work of RAIN. But you can't do that work at times when you're already "outside the window."

To explain what happens when we're overwhelmed by emotion, I like to use another invention of Dan Siegel's—a model of the brain that makes this very complex organ, and our reaction to stress, easier to understand.

THE BRAIN IN THE PALM OF YOUR HAND

Try this at home! Hold up your hand and make a fist with your thumb against your palm and your four other fingers folded tightly down over it. This is your brain. Your face is in front of the knuckles, and the back of your hand is the back of your head.

Now open your fingers again for a moment. Your wrist

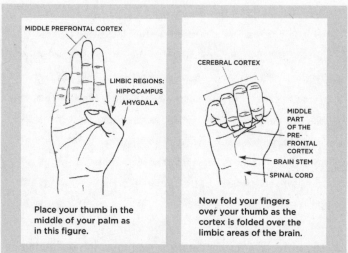

MIDDLE PREFRONTAL CORTEX

LIMBIC REGIONS:
HIPPOCAMPUS
AMYGDALA

Place your thumb in the middle of your palm as in this figure.

CEREBRAL CORTEX

MIDDLE PART OF THE PRE-FRONTAL CORTEX

BRAIN STEM

SPINAL CORD

Now fold your fingers over your thumb as the cortex is folded over the limbic areas of the brain.

represents your spinal cord. Your lower palm is your brain stem. And your curled-in thumb is the limbic area of your brain. The brain stem is responsible for basic bodily functions (like breathing and heart rate), our levels of arousal, and survival reactions like the fight-flight-freeze response. The limbic area, deep within the brain, is our emotional center, and it works closely with the brain stem to drive our actions and responses. (As Siegel explains, the limbic area focuses on the crucial question "Is this good or is this bad?") It's also where our memories are formed and stored. Most of this activity goes on outside our awareness.

If you fold your fingers over your thumb again, you're bringing the top layer of the brain, the cortex, online. This is the most recently evolved part of the brain, which allows us to orient ourselves in space and time, think, reason, plan, and imagine. The prefrontal cortex—the area right behind your forehead—extends from your first knuckles down to your fingertips. Press your fingertips into your palm, and notice that they link together all the parts of your brain. This is the area that sends and receives the messages that guide our lives. The middle prefrontal area is the witness. It has the capacity for mindfulness, empathy, and compassion. It underlies our ability to navigate complex relationships. And it is the domain that can calm or "down-regulate" the survival reactions of the primitive brain.

If you are in a resilient state, communication is flowing between all parts of your brain. (Dr. Siegel calls this state "integration.") Say someone cuts you off while you're driving your child to school. Your limbic system and brain stem react so fast you step on the brakes before you're fully aware of what's happening. Then you feel the surge of fear and anger flooding your entire body. But now the prefrontal cortex sends a calming message: "That was close, but we're out of danger." Gradually, you begin to settle back into your skin.

But if you have been overstressed or traumatized, the prefrontal cortex may not be able to down-regulate the limbic response. Fear and anger take over. You might shout expletives and frighten your child or, worse, try to catch up with the car and pass it or give the driver the finger. When we are hijacked by our survival brain, we can easily harm ourselves and others.

You can see how this works by consulting your hand-model of the brain. The messages "Danger! Trouble!" surge up through your brain stem into your limbic system. And because your prefrontal cortex (the four fingers wrapped around your thumb) is already overstressed, it disengages and your fingers just pop up. You literally "flip your lid"! Your arousal stays sky-high, and you lose access to good judgment, empathy, moral reasoning, and other inner strengths we count on to guide us in living wisely.

When we are cut off from our natural capacity for mindfulness and self-compassion, we need a way of soothing our system so we can reconnect. We need a way back to integration and resilience. This is, once again, when calling on the Nurture step of RAIN is a crucial path to healing.

NURTURING WHEN FEAR IS STRONG

In chapter 5, we explored how the Nurture step of RAIN allows us to work with shame. When we're caught in shame, our deepest need is to trust that we are lovable and valuable. With RAIN, we learn to find a source of love larger than ourselves, a resource that helps us trust our basic goodness.

When fear is pushing us outside our window of tolerance and we are feeling overwhelmed, *our immediate need is to access a sense of safety*. In this case, in order to work with RAIN effectively, we need to feel sufficiently safe and present *before* we begin. This is why I often suggest Nurturing and strengthening your inner resource anchor as a first step. You can also pause to Nurture at any point in the meditation.

You might be wondering, "But I thought the Nurture step was at the end of RAIN?" As we've seen, full Nurturing *is* often the final step, coming after we've Investigated and directly contacted our experience. But the self-compassion implicit in Nurture holds the whole process, and when we're facing trauma or other intense fears, the Allow and Investigate steps may not be wise or even possible. At these times, we need to shift the sequence of RAIN. If we Nurture and establish some degree of safety and connectedness at the start, and again whenever it is needed, RAIN is more likely to unfold in a healing way.

One direct approach to Nurturing is to guide your attention to the body and breath, as in the guided meditation on page 107, at the end of this chapter.

A second approach to Nurturing, introduced in chapter 5, is to identify and access a resource anchor—whatever word, image, object, or gesture helps connect you with the inner resources you most need. Once this associative anchor is established, it gives you a quick and direct point of access, one that you can rely on when you're most "under the line."

But if we hope to make a lasting difference in our lives, it's not enough to just access a positive inner state like safety or peace. We now know that we can deliberately build these temporary states into traits—into enduring expressions of who we are. This process of turning states into traits is a profound expression of self-nurturing.

STATES TO TRAITS

Recall that our survival brain is geared to remember painful experiences more readily than pleasant ones; this is our negativity bias. Even when we can't recall painful events in detail (which often happens with trauma), they remain deep in implicit memory, shaping our expectations, beliefs, and mood—the way we experience ourselves and the world. In contrast, many of our day-to-day positive experiences are quickly forgotten. We retain some high points—those full of emotion and meaning. But most of our moments of feeling relaxed, safe, trusting, successful, and loved are passing states.

Making a desired state into a trait, an enduring quality of our being, requires two basic steps. The first is to "have the experience," either by recognizing it when it arises spontaneously or by purposely eliciting it with a resource anchor. The second is to offer our full, sustained, and immersed attention to that positive state and to the self-sense that arises with it. Psychologist Rick Hanson calls this second step "installation." It gives the positive experience "stickiness," so that it becomes installed in our long-term implicit memory for future retrieval.

This is how what might have been a passing state gradually builds into a trait. By repeatedly having the experience and saturating it with our attention, we are recruiting our brain's neuroplasticity to create a radical shift in how we experience ourselves and our life.

REFLECTION: INSTALLING A POSITIVE STATE

Installing is possible whenever a positive inner state (moments of calm, confidence, love, safety) arises naturally or when we have intentionally evoked the state. Once it's there, do the following:

- Bring your intention, interest, and attention to sustaining the experience, staying with it for at least fifteen to thirty seconds.

- Allow it to fill your body; invite it to become as big as it can be. Involve all your senses: What are you seeing and hearing? How is your body experiencing touch, temperature, energy, movement? Is taste or smell part of the experience?

- Intend that the experience sink into your cells, the way light fills a room, or water soaks into a sponge. Sense that you are letting in the felt experience, surrendering to it, receiving it into yourself.

- Take a few moments to reflect on what feels meaningful or significant about the experience.

The key to successful installation is repetition: accessing and installing over and over. Practice when you're feeling fine, but also when you're grumpy or a bit stressed. Each time you touch a state like peacefulness or strength, let it totally fill you; stay with it for a while. Installing—getting familiar with it—will make it more accessible when you encounter real difficulty.

Whatever you practice grows stronger. Learning how to turn positive states into lasting traits is one of the greatest gifts you can give to yourself. No matter how trapped you've been in emotions like fear or shame, strengthening your inner resources can help change your brain, heal your heart, and evolve your consciousness.

The guided meditations at the end of the chapter—"Nurturing the Seeds of Safety" and "Handing It Over"—will give you a chance to explore this directly.

PRACTICING RAIN WITH OVERWHELMING FEAR

Terry was a long-term meditator, but as her daughter Megan sank into a heroin addiction, Terry became less and less able to find solace in her practice. Instead, sitting in silence often triggered unbearable agitation.

Determined to save her daughter from the streets, Terry had already spent three years on a roller coaster of fear and rage. She'd paid for one rehab center after another. She'd paid for rent, for counseling, tried to find Megan jobs, only to face a continuing web of lies and another relapse. Megan sometimes disappeared for weeks, leaving Terry panicked, and then showed up again when she hit bottom, desperate for help, promising this time would be different.

Terry knew she was enabling addictive behavior, but she couldn't stop. She lived in terror that she'd get a call: Megan was in the morgue after overdosing. Megan had been raped and killed.

It wasn't until her best friend told her, "You're traumatized and you need support for yourself right now," that Terry began therapy and came to me for spiritual guidance.

I asked her what in her life gave her a sense of connectedness and peace. "Usually prayer," she responded. "I pray to what feels like the mother of the universe, the Divine Mother. But now when I try to pray, it's like my heart is buried in fear. I can hardly breathe."

"What would help your heart breathe right now?" I asked.

Terry closed her eyes for a moment. "If I weren't carrying

this fear alone," she said. Then she looked at me with a small smile: "I wish the universe could take over for me!"

"Then let's just go with that," I said. "Okay?" She nodded gamely and again closed her eyes.

"Let the fears you're carrying, the big ones, come to mind. And now imagine that you are holding them gently and respectfully in both hands . . . and placing them into the arms of the Divine Mother. It's not that you're getting rid of them. It's more like letting something much larger help you hold them. See if you can visualize and feel this. You might try actually cupping your hands and lifting them up."

Terry bowed her head slightly as her hands rose. Tears started streaming down her face. Several minutes later, she brought her hands down and sat very quietly. "I'm breathing, Tara," she said. "My heart's breathing. It's unbelievably heavy and sad, but there's more space . . . it's part of something larger . . . it's breathing."

Terry had found a resource anchor (the image and felt sense of that prayerful gesture) that could give her some ease. I encouraged her to sit quietly for a while, resting in the breath, noticing what it was like to let the calm enter and fill her heart. Before we parted, I suggested that she make this the center of her practice—handing over her fears to the Divine Mother (her resource anchor) and then steeping herself in the feelings of being held (to install the inner state).

When fears are deeply entrenched and/or daily life keeps reinforcing them, you might need to cultivate safety for days, weeks, or months *before* going on to full RAIN. And even then, it's important to stop and access your inner resources whenever there are signals of "too much."

When Terry and I met several weeks later, Megan had left another rehab center and was entirely off her mother's radar. Terry was miserable, but she had been praying a lot and said she felt ready to bring the full mindfulness and compassion of RAIN to her experience. I reminded her that she could ask the Divine Mother at any time to help her hold her fear.

She began by Recognizing and Allowing the fear and distress she was feeling. When she started to Investigate and asked herself, "What am I believing?" she heard herself say, "I'm powerless to control her or save her." She paused, and I could see her deepen her breathing. "It's a dark, clutching fist of fear in my chest," she whispered, "and I just have to stay here." Then, after a few moments, she added, "When I sense the Divine Mother helping to hold the fear, it helps."

Terry continued to breathe into that intensity, and something shifted. Tears came, then sobbing, as she curled up on the couch in the fetal position. "I might lose my baby, and there's nothing I can do." Terry had faced the anguish of loss that lived inside the clutch of her fear.

She grieved deeply for about ten minutes, and when she grew quiet, I asked, "What does that grieving place most need?"

She sat up slowly and muttered, "Right now? Water and tissues." She was back in the room with me. After she settled a bit, she said, "It needs to be here, but . . . it's just so big. It needs to be held by all the kindness in the universe. Just like the fear, held by something larger than me."

Again, I invited Terry to take more time, simply letting the grief be there, letting it be held by something larger, resting in her experience. She sat a while, rocking slightly and holding herself. Then she gently cupped her hands and lifted them in offering, bowing her head. After some minutes I asked, "What's it like as you allow this grieving and open to that vast kindness?"

"It's like this great wrenching heartache is floating in a boundless sea of compassion . . . there's some peace."

The roller coaster with Megan wasn't over for Terry, but her inner surrender allowed her to respond with more wisdom. Although it ripped her up, she said no to the next round of Megan's pleas and promises. It became even harder when she found out her daughter was homeless and prostituting herself to support her habit. But Terry knew deeply that she couldn't be Megan's rescuer. Instead, she had to remain open to her own fear and grief and let them be held in that sea of compassion.

Terry's boundaries forced Megan to choose. She chose to live. Over the next four years, she took increasing responsibility for her life, slowly facing the demons she'd been running from.

OUR FEARLESS HEART

In my experience, fear does not stop arising. Our life is inherently insecure: We lose people we love, relationships fail, we fall short in our work life, our bodies will die, our globe will keep erupting in violence, our earth will continue to experience threats to its biosystems and species. Ultimately, we have no control over living and dying.

And yet, as Terry discovered, it is possible to experience the natural contraction of fear with radical compassion. Fear, a changing state, can be held in vast tenderness, a trait expressing our deepest nature. Through the practice of RAIN, we can discover this heartspace—a loving presence larger than our small, frightened self—that includes anxiety or fear without becoming possessed or consumed by it.

When I last saw Terry, she told me what she's learned from the ups and downs: "I can't control Megan's life. . . . She still has big challenges, and I can't make sure everything works out. All I can do is care, do my best to be helpful, and when I'm afraid, try to stay present. If I call on the Divine Mother, there's enough love and presence to hold the fear, to hold my life."

Each of us can learn to Nurture our inner resources, to discover our fearless heart in the face of fear. Our resource anchors may be very different—bringing to mind a trusted friend or a spiritual figure, leaning against a tree, touching our own heart, holding a rock. Yet if we offer our full attention to the positive inner state they awaken, we are directly Nurturing a tender presence that can hold our life.

MEDITATION: NURTURING THE SEEDS OF SAFETY

There are three primary pathways for increasing inner safety through meditation: attention to body and breath; wise and loving messages; and mentally evoking a person, place, activity, or memory.

⊖

1. Body and Breath

- Ground yourself by becoming aware of your body and making sure you are in a stable and comfortable position. Feel how your back, bottom, and feet are pressing the chair or floor; feel your weight and the sense of gravity, how the earth is holding you up.

- Scan your body, and consciously relax whatever tension you find.
- Focus on your breath, slowing to a long in breath and long out breath (approximately five to six seconds each). Breathe without pausing between the inflow and the outflow, relaxing with the outflow and letting the entire breath be smooth and easy. (This is known as "coherence breathing." It directly calms the body and mind.)
- Place your hand(s) gently on your heart, belly, or cheeks.

2. Wise and Loving Messages

- Self-message, such as "I'm here. I'm with you."
- Prayers/blessings of loving kindness: "May I feel safe from inner and outer harm."
- Mantras or phrases with sacred meaning, such as "*Orn Mani Padmi Hum*." (As our minds awaken, we discover the jewel of compassion.)

3. Mentally Evoking a Person, Place, Activity, or Memory

To identify which of these might serve as a good potential resource anchor, reflect on the following questions when you are not in the grip of fear. Pay attention to your body, and notice which most bring you a sense of ease:

- *With whom do you feel connection or belonging? Feel cared for or loved? Feel at home, safe, secure?* You might scan family, friends, teachers, and healers—those you know and also those beings you feel connected to but have never met; those who are living or who have passed; pets; archetypal or spiritual figures like the Buddha, Kwan Yin, Jesus.

- *When and where do you feel most at home—safe, secure, relaxed, or strong?* Here you might consider where you feel a sense of sanctuary—in the natural world, in a church or temple, at home, in a coffee shop.

- *What activity brings a sense of safety, security, and/or strength?* Notice if there is something you do—helping others, swimming, drawing, dancing—that connects you with your inner resources.

- *What events from the past—particular experiences—are reminders of when you've felt strong, safe, and empowered?* This might include any time of accomplishment or mastery, of learning or service, of being in relationship with others.

After reflecting on these questions, choose the person, place, activity, or memory that currently best offers a sense of safety. This is, for now, your resource anchor, your portal to a positive state.

Deepen your attention by bringing this resource anchor alive with all your senses. For example, if it's a person you feel at home with, let the image of the person be clear and close in, remind yourself of sounds and words that might have been spoken, and recall a reassuring touch or look.

. . .

After you access your resource anchor through one of these three pathways, notice the feelings that arise in your body—the felt sense of ease, safety, or comfort.

End your reflection by taking fifteen to thirty seconds to install these positive experiences of safety or security, immersing your attention in the feelings, and letting them sink in and fill you.

MEDITATION: HANDING IT OVER

Explore this meditation whenever you find yourself obsessing, worrying, and anxious about outcomes. Notice what happens when you entrust your difficulties to a larger universe.

—⊖—

Find a comfortable position, close your eyes, and relax any obvious areas of tension.

Take some moments to Recognize and Allow any experience of anxiety or fear. Investigate by sensing what you are believing (what bad thing is going to happen) and by experiencing where the fear is felt most strongly in your body. Deepen the Investigation by directly contacting and opening to the sensations.

Now bring to mind some benevolent entity or formless being—god, spirit, intelligence of the universe, Jesus, Buddha, Divine Mother, Nature—that you sense as wise, compassionate, and all-embracing.

Imagine taking the full mass of the fear you've been carrying and handing it over—offering it into this larger field, this vaster being. It's no longer your "job" to worry or to carry this alone. Your small self is not in charge. Let the fears or worries be held in the hands of something larger.

Visualize and sense the "handing over." You might try enacting it physically, raising both hands toward the heavens and lowering your head. How do you feel when you are not holding the weight of this burden?

After the RAIN: If there is no problem to solve, what is this moment like? See if you can relax and rest in an easeful space.

QUESTIONS AND RESPONSES

When fear arises, am I always supposed to go through the four steps of RAIN?

Not necessarily! There are several ways your practice might unfold:

The first steps of RAIN—Recognize and Allow— often elicit a mindful, open presence that helps us find balance and freedom in the midst of fear (or whatever emotion is difficult). In other words, you might just need the first two steps.

At other times, when the fear is strong and you are caught in reactivity, Investigating will help uncover the layers of vulnerability, and Nurturing will offer the healing that is needed.

Finally, as I've suggested above, when fear is intense, you might need to start with Nurturing, and establish a sufficient sense of safety before moving through the steps of RAIN.

Doesn't "handing over" our fears disempower us? Or reinforce our sense that our fears are too much for us to manage?

When we're stuck in fear, we're *not* handling it well. We already feel victimized, possessed, separate, and vulnerable. The reason is that our survival brain has taken over, reducing communication with our prefrontal cortex, the site of reason, mindfulness, and compassion. And while it might initially seem that we're handing fear over to something outside us, we're actually using our imagination to reconnect with our own resources, our own temporarily hidden wisdom, compassion, and love. "Handing it over" (much like the "Turning it over" encouraged in 12-step programs) can be a powerful bridge back to our wholeness.

How can I tell when I'm outside my window of tolerance? I know there's a danger of re-traumatization, but sometimes I wonder if I'm just avoiding discomfort.

If you have a history of trauma and/or experience PTSD symptoms like nightmares, being easily startled, and strong anxiety or panic, it's best to assume that emotional discomfort or feelings of "too much" mean you are outside your window of tolerance. Otherwise, you can "play your edge" and try to stay present for a while with your discomfort, witnessing it as it unfolds. Then, if the discomfort becomes acute, take that as a signal to shift your attention, and turn to an inner resource for self-soothing. But you may discover that with practice you develop enough balance and resilience to be with your fears. When you learn to stay present, you undo habitual avoidance and gain more ease and freedom in the midst of stress. You actually enlarge your window of tolerance.

I think I'm acting from fear, but when I meditate, I can't find the fear in my body.

You are not alone! We humans have a strong reflex to disassociate from the body's raw experience of fear and retreat into fear-based thinking and behavior. It takes practice to deliberately open yourself to the felt sense of fear. When fearful thoughts arise during meditation, bring a friendly attention to your throat, chest, and belly, breathing into those areas to help you focus. Notice any sensations of tightness, soreness, heat, pressure, or shakiness, and invite the fear to show itself. If you are patient, you will gradually become familiar with how fear expresses itself in your body. And with that familiarity, you will find you are less hooked by fear. You'll be better able to respond to fear, rather than react from it.

Getting in touch with my fears in meditation triggered my PTSD symptoms. I'm afraid I'll fall apart if I continue. Should I keep on meditating?

If you are experiencing PTSD symptoms, it is wise to cultivate more inner resources before continuing with mindfulness and RAIN. Once you have strengthened your access to inner resources, you may find that your window of tolerance increases. Also, it can be very helpful to consult a trauma-sensitive teacher or mindfulness-based therapist about ways to modify your practice.

Keep in mind that there are many types of meditation, and some directly cultivate inner resources of calm and well-being. For example, you may already be familiar with loving-kindness meditation, or concentration on the breath, or a walking practice. Any of these can help you feel more stable and at ease during difficult times.

SEVEN

Discovering Your Deepest Longing

*Men are only free when they are doing what the
deepest self likes. And there is getting down to the
deepest self! It takes some diving.*

⁎ D. H. LAWRENCE

For his sixtieth birthday, Max came with his partner, Paul, to
a daylong workshop titled "Radical Acceptance." Paul had
insisted. "Six decades is enough," he'd said. "You're charging
to the finish line and not taking in the scenery."

Max, the owner of an investment consulting firm, agreed.
"I suffer from FOMO," he confessed, when the three of us
spoke during a break. Seeing my raised eyebrows, he added,
"Fear of Missing Out. I'll hear about something—a new work-
out, the next-gen iPhone, a high school reunion, an amazing
life-changing workshop"—he paused dramatically to smile at
me—"and be afraid I'll miss the boat by not being part of it."

Then he paused again and looked at me with a more serious
expression. "The truth is, I'm anxious and never content. Paul
nailed it last weekend when he asked me, 'What is enough?'

I've got so much going for me—great career, good reputation, health, loving partner—but it never seems enough." Then he added, "My real FOMO is that life's passing by and I'm missing out on what really matters."

Fear of Missing Out. Max and Paul had introduced me to the shorthand for how so many of us live—haunted by the sense that there's never enough time, that we'll die without living fully. Whether we're chasing after the next sensational experience, another person's love, or a drink to soften our fears, in those moments we are missing out on presence. We have left the only place—here and now—where we can realize the truth of who we are, connect caringly with others, and listen to the wind in the trees.

The Zen poet Ryokan wrote, "If you want to find the meaning, stop chasing after so many things." Chronic wanting keeps us from ever really arriving in the moment and seeing it as it is. When we're always on our way somewhere else, we are not living the life that is here.

RAIN helps to free us from the wanting that constricts our life. In this chapter, you'll see how Investigating can reveal the unmet needs that drive unhealthy habits of wanting and how Nurturing connects us with inner wholeness and fulfillment. But first let's look at the universal conditioning that keeps us feeling that something is missing, that this moment is not enough.

AWAY FROM YOUR STAR

Our word "desire" comes from the Latin verb for "missing" or "longing": *desiderare*, which means "being away from the stars."

Consider this: Every part of this universe is made of star stuff; our star is the source of our aliveness; its luminosity reflects awareness itself. All forms arise from that source and suffer when they feel separated from it. With this comes a yearning for connectedness and feeling fully alive. The default focus of desire is pleasure because pleasure is a primal biological signal for that which serves this full aliveness: safety, food, sex, self-worth, connection with others, spiritual realization. Desire, then, is the energy of our star calling us home.

While seeking pleasure can be entirely wholesome, the energy of desire becomes problematic and hard to navigate whenever our basic needs are not met. Then desire intensifies, and our attention narrows and fixates on more attainable or tangible substitutes. If we feel unsafe, we may seek power or money; if we feel unloved, we may constantly seek approval or pile up accomplishments in the hope of winning affection. And if our needs have been radically unmet, our fixations can take over. Desire turns into craving and addictive behavior.

Substitutes provide a temporary fix that keeps us hooked, but they never truly deliver. Our accomplishments never allow us to feel truly worthwhile; our money or possessions do not bring real security; our hundreds of friends on social media will never convince us we are lovable. So we keep feeling that something is missing, reaching for substitutes and distancing ourselves from our star—the source of our longing.

REFLECTION: "IF ONLY" MIND

When we pursue substitutes, we're in a limbic trance; the beliefs and unmet needs driving us are largely "below the line," outside conscious awareness. Investigating reveals a chronic feeling of dissatisfaction that keeps us leaning forward and a belief that "if only" things would change, life would be better.

Is there something on the horizon that (if it happens) you're convinced will make everything different? That you'll be fulfilled or content "if only" you can find the right partner, or have a child, or lose weight, or get the right job—or if your teen gets accepted at the right college? Now investigate the effect of "if only" mind: How does it shape your thoughts and your mood? Your decisions as you navigate life? Your capacity to enjoy your life now? Are you waiting for your life to happen?

Try noticing how "if only" shows up in smaller ways throughout your day: If only I could stay in bed a little longer, the kids would get dressed faster, there was less traffic, I could get another cup of coffee, get this project out of the way, get the latest upgrade for my mobile device, get my files in order, have that glass of wine, have someone else clean up the kitchen, sleep through the night. When you do get what you've been wanting, how long do you stay satisfied?

Now pause your reading, and check this moment for hints of "if only." Is there a sense that you are on your way to something else? A background feeling of dissatisfaction? Is there something missing right now?

Because substitutes never satisfy for long, the waves of fixated desire can take over our lives. We are tossed around on the surface of the sea and unable to access the depths—the pure longing of our deepest self. As D. H. Lawrence says, this takes some diving!

RAIN WITH FOMO

Max's takeaway from our workshop was a relationship with his future self. During a guided meditation, he saw an older version of himself on a small sailboat, carried by the winds around a pristine lake. He wasn't chasing anything or proving anything. The message from his future self was this: "You can be content right where you are."

This vision inspired Max, but it seemed worlds away from his real life. When he came to a retreat four months later, we decided to bring RAIN to what he now called "my endless pursuit." During his sittings, he'd been obsessing on a major new investment, which kept him from coming into presence. I suggested he Recognize and Allow the obsessing and then make the U-turn. "If you shift your attention from your thoughts about the project to the feelings in your body, what do you notice?" He named "excitement, grasping, and fear."

Further investigation revealed an area of heat, pressure, and agitation in his chest. I asked what that place was believing, and he said, "That if I don't do something, I'll miss out. I'll lose my chance."

"What will you lose?" I asked.

Max shook his head. "I don't know, maybe money? A chance to do good? An impressive addition to my résumé?"

"Is it true, Max? Will you lose something important?"

Again he shook his head. "No, but that's how it feels. And that's how it always feels . . . that if I don't act, I'll lose something . . . lose aliveness, life."

Now that he had contacted the mix of fear and wanting as a felt experience in his body, I suggested that Max again bring to mind his future self as a source of wise Nurturing. "How might your future self guide you?"

He nodded and after a few minutes said, "I'm on that sailboat with him, but this time it's different. He's actively engaging the wind, however it's blowing. He's present, alive . . . having a blast!" Max was smiling.

I asked, "Is there something he wants you to know?"

"Totally. It's like he just put a hand on my shoulder and said, 'Life is enough in this moment. You don't have to chase things. *This* is it!'" Then he opened his eyes and laughed. "It's right now, Tara, . . . riding these winds . . . sitting here, breathing, exploring this stuff with you, feeling warmth in my chest. *This* is *it*!"

Especially if we've been chasing after something outside ourselves, when we contact what's happening right now, we might find, as Max did, the agitation or tension or fear that's part of desire. Often there's a nagging sense of "something's missing." But what happens if instead of pursuing what we think we want, we stay there? What happens if we encourage ourselves (as with a kind hand on our shoulder) to trust that "this is it"? Gradually we will discover the fullness and aliveness of our own presence. With this comes the blessing of feeling "enough"—

that what we really long for is already here. We can feel the spirit of this in a famous poem by the Zen master Ryokan: "The thief left it behind: the moon at the window."

It's important to remember that while coming into presence frees us inwardly, it doesn't necessarily mean radical outward change. Max's daily activities stayed pretty much the same. Laid-back wasn't really his style. He continued competing for high-profile contracts and the esteem of professional colleagues. But as he put it, "I'm not so restless and driven . . . there are more times when I'm really here. And when I do start anxiously chasing after a better wind, the old sailor puts a hand on my shoulder and whispers, 'This is it!'"

ADDICTED TO LOVE

The medicine for Max's FOMO was learning to keep coming back to the present moment. Yet there are times when we cannot make the U-turn into presence without encountering deep and raw layers of unmet needs. I've seen this in my own life, and with countless others, when desire snowballs into full-blown obsession. At these times, we need to pay deeper attention to the craving and fear that are driving us.

David came to a meditation retreat shortly after his partner of six months ended their volatile romance. He was tormented by her loss. His mind kept raking through their short history, rerunning moments of passion, moments when their love seemed to promise a lifetime of intimacy together. The more he obsessed, the more desperate his longing became.

When we met privately, he proclaimed, "I've lost the love

of my life. People keep telling me I'll find someone else, someone even better, but . . . I don't believe it. I think she was the one. I feel like my life is over."

David was surprised when I suggested that we do RAIN together, starting right where he was. The words poured out: "I sit there trying to meditate, and all I can think about is calling her, making up, making love, making it work." He told me how he kept going over their last fight in his head, trying to figure out exactly how he'd screwed up.

"What feeling are you most aware of?" I asked.

"Wanting," he said, "intense, nonstop wanting."

"See if you can just Recognize this wanting and Allow it to be there, without adding any judgment." He shook his head with disgust. "That's hard. I feel so out of control, so ashamed that I'm wanting her so badly."

"I understand, David. That's so natural. See if you can Allow that too, the shame that comes with the wanting. It might help to name these feelings—'wanting, wanting . . . shame, shame'—and just pause, giving them space to be here for now."

After a few moments, he nodded, and I asked, "What is the strongest emotion right now?"

He didn't hesitate: "Wanting. Every cell in me is yearning to have her back."

"Okay," I said, "then let's Investigate the wanting. Try watching one of your fantasies as if it were playing on a mental screen." I waited as he closed his eyes. "Now notice what happens when you turn away from the screen. What's going on in your body and heart?" After a few moments, I added, "Where does the wanting live in your body? Can you tell me how it feels?" I was encouraging him to make the critical U-turn from thoughts to feelings, to enter his experience fully.

David's wanting turned out to be a clawed hand, nails sunk deep into his heart, yanking. Every tug felt as if it were shredding flesh. His heart was being ripped apart.

We then began to deepen presence through a way of Investigating that I call "Tracing Back Desire." This helps us find the unmet needs and, within them, the true longing that fuels our fixated wants.

"Imagine that you could go inside that wanting energy, that clawed hand that's yanking at your heart." David was leaning forward, his jaws clenched, face scrunched in utter concentration. I waited a few moments, then asked, "What does that wanting energy want to experience?"

"It wants company . . . it doesn't want to be alone."

"Okay, stay inside that yanking feeling," I said, "and sense . . . what is the feeling of 'company'? If it had 'company,' what would that be like?"

"It could relax . . . it could let go . . . it would be part of something."

"And what would it feel like to be 'part of something'? . . . What's that like?"

"It's like"—he put both hands on his chest—"my heart's this open space . . . it's totally alive . . . filled with warmth . . . light."

"Can you feel that right now?" He nodded. "Is this what that wanting energy really wants? Is there anything else?"

David was very still. Then he whispered, "Right now there's no wanting . . ."

Investigation opened into the fullness of Nurture as David rested in this warm, luminous space. After a while, I asked him to sense what he wanted to remember about this experience. "This is love, Tara . . . and it's already here," he responded. David's hands were still on his heart. "But I know I'm going to leave this room, and within minutes or hours I'm going to forget and want it with her." Then, gently patting his chest, he said, "Somehow I have to remember that it's here."

Before we ended our session, we talked about not fighting the fantasies that would inevitably recur, and I told David he should try not to judge himself for this deeply grooved and very human way of seeking love. When we judge our desires, we block the pathway to the love that's buried within the longing, the intrinsic, timeless love that is calling to us.

IS ATTACHMENT BAD?

Many people ask me if we are supposed to let go of our longing for intimate connection with others. They've heard that "attachment" is unhealthy or that it blocks spiritual development. But it's natural and healthy to seek close, nurturing relationships. Our bodies and brains seek attachment from the moment we're born; that's how we humans survive. Infants attach even to caregivers who fail again and again to meet their needs. The challenge is that when our attachment needs haven't been met in early life, we may grasp after intimacy—or push it away—making real connection impossible. And when our substitutes fall short, we often touch the feelings of abandoned children everywhere, crying in the night for comfort that doesn't come.

For David, passionate sex simply upped the ante. We humans have been struggling with (and celebrating) the biology of desire ever since we came down out of the trees. Hormones and other neurotransmitters flood the body, driving both arousal and bonding and creating a strong imprint on memory. Some of the same brain circuits are also involved in addiction to opiates and other drugs. No wonder David felt a claw in his heart; he was in withdrawal.

That's why the process David was learning—finding a love sourced within—is essential for healing. When desire is outwardly fixated, RAIN helps us undo the fixation by making the U-turn into our direct experience. Attachment will still arise; it just won't run our lives and block the flow of love. The more we can trust the loving inside ourselves, the more we can connect with others from a place of wholeness, spontaneity, and authentic care.

FROM UNMET NEEDS TO ADDICTION

If our earliest needs for safety and connection have not been met, we become more susceptible to addiction. Neuroscientists have documented that stress causes biological changes in the brain, including a decrease in the dopamine receptors that register pleasure. This makes us more driven to seek high-intensity rewards involving sex, food, money, or drugs. While we can get a fix and temporarily light up our pleasure centers, the dopamine receptors become less sensitive, and we need more and more stimulation to get satisfaction. As participants in Alcoholics Anonymous are sometimes reminded, "One drink may make you feel like a new person . . . then the new person has to have a drink."

When we're caught in craving, activity in the prefrontal cortex decreases. This impairs critical thinking and capacity for restraint. You feel like an entirely different person. It's you in limbic hijack, without access to your more recently evolved brain! Over time, the brain patterns that make up our self-sense become deeply disrupted. Our thinking, our feelings, our choices, and our ways of relating to others all become hitched to the addiction. We lose contact with the gold—the spirit that animates our being.

SUBSTITUTING FOOD FOR LOVE

Fran came to see me on the recommendation of her sponsor at Overeaters Anonymous, a 12-step group. She told me OA was helping. Making new friends, hearing their struggles, and honestly sharing her own helped her feel less ashamed of her compulsion to eat. But whenever Fran hit a major stressor, she still relapsed into bingeing.

Maybe she was missing a key ingredient, she said. "The people who believe in a higher power have someplace to turn when they're alone and the going gets tough, but I don't. My sponsor has tried to help me with this. I can sense there's something larger than me in this universe, but not some godlike power watching over me in particular."

Fran wanted to know if meditation could give her the inner strength to resist her compulsion to eat. I suggested we start with RAIN and asked if she was willing to revisit a recent episode of bingeing.

"Oh, that would be when my father and stepmother were coming," she said. Fran told me they had a strained relationship and that she'd been dreading their visit. She'd gotten home from work early to clean house, snacked instead of having dinner, and then the snacking turned into an extended binge on cereal and ice cream.

She said that her anxiety had really kicked in as she converted her office into a guest room and tried to plan a meal they'd enjoy. We began RAIN there, with Fran noting that anxiety and pausing to give it some space. She Investigated by asking that anxious place what it was believing. "Well, they're going to regret coming, they'll think my pullout couch isn't comfortable and that I can't cook. They'll compare me to my older brother and sister, who are earning over 200K a year each and have families and live a more traditional lifestyle . . ."

"Okay . . . so let's slow down and take a moment," I said. "What is the strongest feeling that is coming up?"

"Anxiety . . . but also . . . well, really, hurt. In their mind, I'm a loser; they don't respect me."

"And when you let yourself feel that hurt . . . where is it in your body?"

Fran put a hand on her throat. "Right here," she said. "My throat feels strangled . . . like I'm trying to hold back tears, hold back words."

"What would happen if you stopped holding back tears and words?"

"If all that pain came out, no one would ever want to be

around me." She paused, then continued: "My brother always used to tell me, 'You're hurt waiting to happen.' Even when I was very little." Fran started crying. "Nobody wants to be with me when I'm hurting."

"Is that really true?"

"Well . . . I don't want to be with me. . . . I feel so childlike, so stupid for being so sensitive."

I asked Fran to go inside that place in her throat that felt strangled, that young place that so easily felt hurt. "What does that part most need from you right now . . . how does it want you to be with it?"

"It wants me to know that it's hurting, and it wants me to care, and . . . not to leave."

"Okay, now take a few moments here, Fran, and let yourself witness that hurting place from the kindest, wisest part of your being. . . . How do you want to respond?"

Fran sat a bit taller and took a few deep breaths. "I want to assure that young part that I care. . . . I do care . . . but I know I will leave. I just can't stay with those feelings for long."

"How about telling her that you care, and you want to stay, even though it's hard, and you'll do the best you can?"

Fran nodded. "The hurting place said that's good enough." And after a time she added, "Something inside me is easier . . . just tender, not hurting as much."

HOLE IN THE SOUL

"I was born with what I like to call a hole in my soul. . . . A pain that came from the reality that I just wasn't good enough. That I wasn't deserving enough. That you weren't paying attention to me all the time. That maybe you didn't like me enough.

"For us addicts, recovery is more than just taking a pill or maybe getting a shot. . . . Recovery is also about the spirit, about dealing with that hole in the soul."

—*William Cope Moyers*

Over the next several months, Fran and I did many rounds of RAIN together. The Investigation step helped Fran become intimately familiar with the unmet need for belonging—for being seen, cared for, accompanied. Contacting the "hole in her soul" that was driving her anxiety made it easier for her to send herself messages of care. But outside our sessions, when the anxiety progressed to compulsion, she was unable to stay present in that hurting place. She'd interrupt the old pattern briefly and then just roll into a binge.

This began to change after a RAIN meditation she did on her own. When we next met, Fran told me she'd felt hurt when an OA friend didn't include her in a post-meeting outing. Her adult mind knew it was probably an innocent oversight, but her inner child was wounded. Typically, she would have gone home and (as she put it) stuffed the child with food. But this time she went directly into her bedroom and curled up in bed. Her hands went to her throat, and soon she was sobbing. "It was like I was utterly alone, young, no one there . . . and at the same time I was also watching. My heart just opened to this young girl, and I whispered over and over, 'I want to be with you, I'm not leaving, I'm not leaving.' And then it wasn't even me whispering. It was like my soul . . . this light-filled presence . . . was embracing her . . . me . . . I don't know. But it was spiritual, beyond the little me. I guess this is my higher power . . . even when all the emotions settled, I felt like I was glowing."

YOUR STAR IS CALLING YOU

That glow Fran experienced in After the RAIN was empowering. Within days, she was able to interrupt what might have been a damaging relapse. She accepted that sometimes she'd still get hooked and that cultivating this pathway would be a lifetime's work. But she now trusted that—together with the support of OA—she could respond to the needs of the hurting part within her. Nurturing and staying present during After the RAIN would deepen her connection with that caring presence she called her soul. It also shifted a deeply lodged, limiting sense of identity. As Fran said, "I have addictive behaviors, but I am not an addict. . . . I'm so much more."

Awakening from the trance of wanting is a spiritual path. When you are driven by unmet needs to pursue harmful substitutes, you are being driven further and further from your star. The suffering of wants and addictive cravings is your star calling you to awaken, and RAIN can guide you in listening and responding. You can learn to make the U-turn, discover what you really long for, and heal your unmet needs. Through the radical compassion of RAIN, you can discover the timeless, loving source that has been calling you home.

MEDITATION:
TRACING BACK DESIRE

Sit comfortably, and take a few full breaths, releasing tension and letting go with the out breath.

Scan your life and sense where the energy of wanting might be taking over in some way and causing suffering.

Bring to mind a particular situation that might regularly trigger the desire or the thoughts that most stimulate this wanting. Let the situation or thoughts be as clear and close as possible so you can feel the wanting alive inside you.

Recognize and Allow the wanting to be there, and if there is a layer of judgment ("I shouldn't be feeling this"), see if it's possible to send a gentle message that this is a natural, universal experience. "It belongs."

Investigate the desire by letting your physical posture express wanting, perhaps by leaning forward, clenching your fists, feeling how your face is when wanting is strong. Then bring your attention inside your body: Where do you feel the energy of wanting? What sensations are you most aware of? Are they pleasant or unpleasant? Is there fear? Any other emotion?

Now continue Investigating by asking that wanting place, "What do you most long for right now?" Attention? Safety? Acceptance? Connection? Understanding? Love? Listen, and then, whatever the response, ask, "Imagine if you received that, what would that give you, what would that be like?"

Often it can take repeating the question—"Imagine if you received that, what would that give you, what would that be like?"—in order to contact within yourself the experience you are longing for.

With each round, try to feel in your body what the experience you are wanting really is. What would it actually feel like if you got the love (understanding, connection, belonging) you long for?

Nurture by giving yourself permission to open to and fill yourself with the goodness of this experience. Soak it into every cell, and rest in the experience you are longing for.

After the RAIN: You might ask yourself, "Is it true that what I long for is already here?"

MEDITATION: WHAT IS MY DEEPEST LONGING?

Find a comfortable way of sitting, and allow yourself to relax and be at ease. With a receptive presence, become aware of the state of your heart. Is there a sense of openness or tightness? Of peace or anxiety? Of contentment or dissatisfaction? As you feel the region of your heart, direct the breath there, so you are gently breathing in and out of your heart.

Begin to Investigate by asking yourself, "What does my heart really long for?" It can also be helpful to ask, "What most matters in this life?" Or, "If I was at the end of my life looking back, what would be most important about how I lived today . . . this moment?" As you pose these questions, sense that you are addressing your inquiry directly to your heart.

After asking, simply listen and be aware of any words, images, or feelings that arise. Try to be patient. It can take some time for the mind to open out of its habitual ideas about life and connect with what is most alive and true. You may need to repeat, several times, some version of "What does my heart long for?" and then listen in receptive silence. As you listen, stay in touch with the feelings in your body, and particularly in your heart.

Your longing will probably express itself differently at different times. You might feel an aspiration to love fully or to feel loved, to know truth, to be peaceful, to be helpful, to be free from fear and suffering. There is no "right" longing. Sometimes you will land on an immediate intention that supports your longing. For example, you might become aware of the yearning to write poetry, to practice yoga, to help others, to engage in social activism. This would be in service of the deep longing to live a creative, compassionate, vital life. What is important is attuning to what is most true for you in this moment.

The sign of arriving at a deep longing is a felt sense of sincerity, innocence, energy, or flow. Some people describe an inner shift that gives them fresh resolution, openness, and ease. If there is no real sense of connecting with what matters, that's fine. You might sit quietly and open to whatever comes up or choose to continue this exploration at another time.

After the RAIN: If you sense you've arrived at what feels like a pure and deep longing, allow yourself to let go into its fullness. Feel the very essence of this yearning in your cells as it expresses itself through your whole body and being. Sense the longing as the calling of your awakening heart.

QUESTIONS AND RESPONSES

When I try Tracing Back Desire, I keep arriving at wanting to be special to someone. Is there something wrong with wanting this? If so, where am I supposed to go from here?

We are social animals, and our survival and flourishing rely, in part, on the nurturing of others. It's entirely natural to want to feel special, to want to be treated in certain ways, to want a particular person as a partner. Yet this wanting can cause suffering if it takes over. Our attention becomes fixated on an external source, as if who we are and our entire well-being depended on someone relating to us in a certain way. The purpose of Tracing Back Desire is to connect you with an inner source so that your wants motivate you but don't control and limit your life.

When you're practicing with Tracing Back Desire and you arrive at the desire to be special to someone, deepen your investigation. Make the U-turn by shifting your attention from the person you want (real or imagined) and starting to imagine and explore the inner experience of "feeling special." If you were special to someone, how would that make you feel inside? Warm? Relaxed? Glowing? Vibrant? Connected to everything?

Whatever positive feeling you find—perhaps "warmth and aliveness"—let it fill you. Get familiar with it. This is what you are really wanting; this is the felt sense of being special. And it's here inside you. Get to know and trust this inner source of well-being. You will naturally feel the urge to find that special person as well, and that's fine. But if you know that what you long for can also be found within, you will create much more ease, grace, and contentment in your life.

I know that desire is "natural," but I feel deeply ashamed of how much I crave food, sex, or getting high on drugs.

Most of us believe we should be able to control ourselves and that our cravings mean we're failing—particularly when we act on them. This shame fuels the core sense of deficiency that often drives addictive behavior.

The beginning of freedom is to bring a healing attention to our shame. When we are deprived, craving is natural. If you haven't eaten for a long time, your body will crave food. Similarly, if we are deprived of love, attention, and security, we will crave fulfillment of these universal needs. And if those needs go unmet, that craving will transfer itself to a substitute like food, sex, or drugs. It's not your fault that you have unmet needs and that they are driving you to substitute gratifications. Countless humans are in the same boat.

When shame comes up, try calling on the wisest, most loving part of your being—your future or evolved self. See through those compassionate eyes, and tell your small self, "It's not your fault." Or try saying, "You're okay, sweetheart," or "These cravings are yours, but they are not all of you." And remind yourself, "Others feel this too." If you bring a compassionate presence to shame over and over again, it will gradually loosen its grip. And you will find yourself able to respond to the cravings in a fresh and resourceful way.

PART III

RAIN and Your Relationships

EIGHT

A Forgiving RAIN

I imagine one of the reasons people cling to their hates so stubbornly is because they sense, once hate is gone, they will be forced to deal with the pain.

◦ JAMES BALDWIN

Forgiveness does not change the past, but it does enlarge the future.

◦ PAUL BOESE

A woman from our meditation community who volunteered at a hospice gave me this story about a patient she had befriended.

Charlotte was often anxious or depressed, and as she neared death, she was increasingly mute due to the tumor growing in her throat. One morning when I arrived, I found her distraught from a nightmare: She had dreamed that the staff told her she had only three days to live. Her voice weak and raspy, Charlotte insisted that she wasn't ready, she couldn't die yet. She had something important to say to her husband first. Much to my astonishment, three days later Charlotte was packed and about to go home. The staff told me her tumor had shrunk dramatically.

The next time I visited, Charlotte had returned. She seemed deeply at peace. Here's what she shared with me, as close to her words as I can recall: "I was angry at my husband, on his case, all through our years together. His work and tennis always came before me, he was too permissive with our kids, he was always intellectualizing but couldn't express feelings, couldn't fix things around the house . . . and the list goes on. After twenty-some years of our marriage, he became too close with another woman. He was honest about it and didn't sleep with her, but I never got over it. I guess I already felt rejected. Even from the early days, I couldn't forgive him for not making me feel special. What I saw was a guy who was letting me down, not on my side. I forgot his basic decency and care. It wasn't until that dream that I realized I needed to tell him I loved him . . . that I regretted nothing more in my whole life than how my judgments drove us apart. So I told him and he listened. He shared some of his own regrets, and when we hugged, we both had tears streaming down our cheeks. It was the first closeness we'd had in years. Now I am ready to go."

We don't have to wait until we're dying to free our hearts from the coils of resentment, anger, and blame. Yet because these habits of aggression are so deeply ingrained, we do have to be dedicated and purposeful in order to release them. Otherwise, we risk spending decades in a trance that keeps us from feeling truly close or intimate with anyone, including ourselves.

REFLECTION: AT THE END OF LIFE

I often invite students to imagine they are at the end of their life look-ing back. This vantage point helps us remember what matters most so that we can Recognize the habits that separate us from each other.

—⊖—

Take a few moments now to travel into the future and imag-ine yourself close to death. Now, as if you were looking back through the years, reflect on an important relationship. Was there openness, acceptance, and care? Or were you distanced by judgment, anger, and blame? If you were with this person right now, how might this end-of-life perspective guide you?

Witnessing how resentment ensnares our heart moves us toward a path of forgiving in small and large ways. Like Char-lotte, we most deeply want to be loving and free. There is a wisdom in us that knows that we need to release blame if we are to love each other and love our life.

HEALTHY ANGER VERSUS
THE TRANCE OF BLAME

We've all been wounded by others—neglected, not seen, re-jected, disrespected. Many of us—and those we love—have been abused or devalued and systemically oppressed because of our sexual orientation, gender identity, race, or religion. Anger has an intelligence; it is an essential survival emotion. We need to pay attention when it mobilizes our bodies and fills our minds with stories of wrongdoing. It alerts us to marshal our energies against obstacles to our well-being, to create better boundaries, to defend ourselves from physical threats, to make our needs or views heard when we've been silenced.

And on a societal level, anger in response to oppression can energize the call for justice. Yet, as Buddhist teacher and author Ruth King writes, "anger is not transformative, it is initiatory." It's an energy we need to use wisely.

But what if our stories of blame go on and on? What if we regularly feel triggered, victimized, and angry and our blame is directed toward all sorts of people, including ourselves?

Chronic blame and resentment almost always signal a painfully limiting trance. As the "on button" becomes jammed, our anger hardens into armor around our heart. Like a scab that never falls off, it prevents the light and warmth of awareness from healing our wounds. It leads us to react from fear rather than respond to our circumstances with wisdom. And it separates us from others, undermining understanding, empathy, and intimacy.

When we are in trance, we become what one of my friends calls "blame ready to happen." Like heat-seeking missiles, we're easily triggered by a tone of voice, an offhand comment, being kept waiting, a lack of attention. Our reaction is out of proportion to what is occurring, and we habitually assume that others are judging us, taking advantage of us, disrespecting us, or pushing us away. Or we may nurse slow-burning resentment; perhaps our teen neglects household tasks, or our partner spends too much time working. This chronic resentment is insidious; it creates an unseen distance that gets in the way of loving and enjoying others.

REFLECTION: BLAME READY
TO HAPPEN

When we're in trance, we are easily triggered by situations and people that are associated, often unconsciously, with our original wounds. Awakening from trance begins with recognizing when we are inside it—when our thoughts and feelings are operating "under the line," outside conscious awareness.

While it's natural to be annoyed or hurt by certain behaviors directed toward us, the trance of blame produces a stronger, more painful, and more lasting response. Ask yourself these questions: "How regularly am I triggered?" "When I'm blaming someone, does it take over my whole experience of them?"

With these questions in mind, notice your reaction in situations when people

- criticize you
- don't listen or seem interested when you're talking
- say they're too busy to see you
- don't respond to emails or texts
- let you down—don't help you enough or do "their part"
- don't show you appreciation
- demand too much from you
- disagree with you
- have something you want (wealth, job, home, children, partner)
- are always late

When we're caught in the trance of anger and blame, our survival brain shapes every dimension of our experience. Our bodies are tense, our hearts numb or constricted; our thinking is agitated and rigid. The thicker the trance, the less we have access to our prefrontal cortex, the home of reason, mindfulness, and empathy.

This cutoff from our whole brain dramatically impacts how we perceive others. Rather than real beings with subjective feelings like ourselves, they become what I call Unreal Others. Our attention focuses on their faults, their difference from us, on how they are threatening or impeding us. At the same time, our self-sense narrows and we become an Unreal Self—identified as a victim, identified with our righteous anger. When the aperture of our attention contracts in this way, we are living below the line, unable to feel connected with others or at home with ourselves.

THE UNREAL OTHER

Stefan, a meditation student in our D.C. community, had been trapped for decades in a relationship of Unreal Othering with his father. While aware of how his armoring of blame closed his heart, he felt stymied by the intensity of his resentment and anger.

A sensitive, artistic child who took after his mother in many ways, Stefan knew from an early age that he was a disappointment to his father. His father, who loved carpentry, sports, and all things outdoors, took every opportunity to deride Stefan's lack of athletic ability, his fear of rock climbing, his total lack of interest in tools. At first Stefan strived to find ways to please his dad, but as an adolescent he learned to shut him out, and even stopped talking to him for several months.

The hostility continued after Stefan left home. At holiday gatherings, his father seemed compelled to fling out taunts about the son who couldn't change the oil, who never went to a Patriots game, who didn't like steak. The jabs still drew blood, bringing up the feelings of inferiority and self-doubt that had plagued Stefan since childhood. And while the critiques subsided somewhat after Stefan and his wife had children, and again after Stefan's mother died, the tense distance between the two remained.

Then, a few months before Stefan came to one of our weeklong meditation retreats, his father had a heart attack. He'd been living alone, but now he was forced to move to an assisted-living center. He could no longer drive, and the loss of independence and home devastated him. Stefan helped his sister make the arrangements, but he was unsympathetic. His sister challenged him: "He was a real jerk when you were younger, but that's history. The guy's having a hard time. When are you going to forgive him . . . after he's dead?"

Outraged, Stefan responded, "He'll never know how much suffering he's caused. . . . He doesn't deserve my forgiveness."

Stefan and his father were at a poignant impasse. Both were trapped in their roles: the unsatisfactory son; the hostile, belittling father. Both had hardened into Unreal Others, two-dimensional characters in each other's inner movies, rather than real, complicated, subjective beings with their own passions and cares, hurts and insecurities. Both were relating from the narrow confines of an Unreal Self.

REFLECTION: UNREAL OTHER
AND UNREAL SELF

Bring to mind a recent conflict with a friend, partner, or family member. Now view this as a movie, including what triggered the conflict, and then freeze the frame at a high point of tension.

—⊖—

In those moments, what are you focused on? Is it a facial expression communicating anger or vengefulness, aversion or disrespect? Words or a tone of voice conveying those emotions?

Are you seeing them as a bad, Unreal Other?

What happens when you consider the challenges they face? Might they be feeling hurt, stressed, anxious, deficient, upset with themselves?

What happens when you remind yourself of the things you value about them—the ways they can be caring, helpful, creative, engaging?

Now shift your attention to yourself:

From the perspective of a witness, how do you imagine you look when you are caught in blame? How do you sound? How does your body feel? Your heart? Are you in the role of angry or hurt victim? Self-righteous judge? Threatening aggressor?

Do you like yourself this way? Is this who you really are?

What are you forgetting about your own pain and vulnerability?

What are you forgetting about your goodness, about what really matters to your heart?

When we unconsciously perceive people as bad, Unreal Others, it's easy to hurt them. We no longer see them as the subjective, feeling beings that we are. And as I'll discuss in chapter 10, this Unreal Othering is also the tragic grounds for oppressing whole groups of people whom we deem inferior, dangerous, or hostile because of characterizations such as race or class, religion or political views, and sexual orientation or identity. Still less recognized: our Unreal Othering and violence toward non-human species.

The good news is that our evolving brains have the capacity for mindfulness and compassion. We can emerge from trance, we can see ourselves and others more clearly, and we can cultivate a forgiving heart.

DEFINING FORGIVENESS

Here's a helpful definition: Forgiving means letting go of the protective armor of blame and/or hatred that encases your heart.

Another definition I like is this: Forgiving means never putting anyone (including yourself) out of your heart.

And another: Forgiveness is the compassion that arises when we've brought full presence to the suffering of hurt and wounds.

However, for many the word "forgiveness" does not resonate, or it creates confusion. If this is the case for you, feel free to substitute "compassion" or "openhearted acceptance" for forgiveness as you continue reading.

Forgiveness is a process that unfolds over time. In both myself and others, I've noticed that forgiving often becomes possible after we ourselves have been the recipient of another's kindness. As I reflect on this, it makes sense. When we are treated with compassion, that offering of warmth and connection decreases our fear, reduces our sensitivity to rejection, soothes our wounds, and helps us accept the feelings of loss that lie just under the armor of blame. Our heart begins to soften, and our view expands. We can see more clearly how another might be suffering.

But we don't have to wait for someone else to unlock our heart. Forgiving can unfold through the practice of RAIN, when we use Investigation to look beneath our armor and bring self-compassion to what we find. This too softens our hearts and enables us to extend our compassion to others.

For most people, the shift from blaming others to an inner-directed presence isn't easy. It takes courage to open ourselves to emotional reality, to accept our hurt, fear, and loss. As the writer Anne Lamott once wrote, quoting an unknown source, "Forgiveness is giving up all hope of having had a different past." We are taking the exquisite risk, shedding the protection we've held so tightly, and saying—gently and tenderly—YES to what is.

REFLECTION: WHY DO WE HOLD SO TIGHTLY TO BLAME?

Please bring to mind someone toward whom you often feel anger and blame. Then ask yourself, "If I let go of judging this person as bad or wrong, what painful feeling would I have to feel?"

—⊖—

When I introduce this reflection in workshops, I often ask people to say out loud a word or phrase for what they feel. Hands go up, and person after person shares the fears and vulnerability that lie beneath the armoring of blame. Do any of the following resonate with you?

- Powerless, out of control
- Afraid—they would just go on hurting me
- If they're not wrong, then I'm the one who is wrong
- Hurt
- I'd have to take responsibility
- Accepting a painful loss
- Grief
- I'd have to accept that life isn't fair
- Unlovable
- Unsafe

Forgiving is hard because we'll do almost anything to avoid the vulnerability inside us. It's also hard because we often fear that forgiving means excusing harmful behavior: "You hurt me, but it's okay. I forgive you, so you don't need to take any responsibility." Because forgiving is so central to freeing our own heart and healing our world, I'd like to name some other points that students find confusing.

MISUNDERSTANDINGS ABOUT FORGIVENESS

Forgiving Does Not Mean We Should Deny or Suppress Our Anger or Fear, Hurt or Grief

Our body, heart, and mind naturally contract defensively when we feel hurt, and there's intelligence to that contraction. The message of anger and blame is this: "I'm threatened; there is an obstacle to my well-being." Before moving toward forgiveness, we need to protect ourselves from any imminent danger. We also need to offer acceptance and compassionate presence to whatever emotions we experience. Bypassing an emotion like hate or anger by ignoring or pushing it away can lead to what I call premature forgiveness; we might assume we've forgiven, but actually we've dissociated from the very feelings that need our attention.

If we've experienced abuse or other forms of trauma, it is particularly important to respect the message of anger and take whatever time we need to find a safe space for healing. The idea that we can and "should" forgive a perpetrator may bring up shame and failure, and divert from the natural healing process. Rather than trying to access compassion for another, our full attention needs to be on what gives us a feeling of efficacy and strength. This means feeling our anger, honoring the need for protection, and offering ourselves self-compassion and care. When we've healed enough to be able to think about the person who perpetrated the trauma without being retriggered, we can begin to include them as a Real Other in our heart.

Forgiving Is Not Condoning Harmful Behavior; nor Does It Mean Passivity or Inaction

When we forgive, we are in no way saying "What you did is okay" or that we'll allow the behavior to continue. If a friend betrays our confidence, we can forgive and also create new boundaries, no longer sharing what feels private. We can forgive an ex-partner for emotional abuse and choose never again to be alone with them. We can forgive a therapist or teacher for unethical or harmful behavior and also inform the proper authorities, as well as other people who might be at risk.

While the energy of anger may catalyze us, it can't sustain us in the long run. We need forgiveness to go hand in hand with a deep dedication to social activism. We can forgive politicians who are responsible for destroying our earth's ecosystem and throw ourselves into supporting the movements and leaders that reflect our values. We can release hatred or blame toward those who perpetuate the oppression of marginalized people and devote ourselves to reducing bias and seeking justice and reparation for those who are being harmed.

Forgiving Does Not Have to Be Done on Our Own

We often need support, especially if we've experienced traumatic wounding. We might choose trauma therapy, work with a healer or spiritual counselor, or share with trusted friends. When an entire group has been traumatized—such as those who've lost friends and family in a church bombing, in a shooting rampage, or in war—help often comes first through a collective sharing of fear and grief, through ritual and prayer, and through the powerful and healing experience of belonging to something larger, a fellowship of kindred spirits.

Forgiving Is Rarely a One-Shot or Quick Process

Cultivating a forgiving heart—in response to both deep violations and small grievances—is a lifelong process. Like physical healing, it has its own organic timing and can't be rushed. Especially when we have deep wounds, healing happens in stages: We often need to bring a caring attention to unfolding layers of anger, fear, shame, and grief.

For many people, blame and resentment are strongest in our closest, most significant relationships. This means we are apt to be continually retriggered. You might find that every time your partner seems at all judgmental, you contract into a frightened, angry, armored self. You may have to move through many rounds of connecting with the hurt under your armor, nurturing yourself, and letting go of the anger. As you do, you'll find that each round helps to heal your woundedness; each round empowers you; each round gives you a larger sense of who you are and makes it more possible to live without pushing others out of your heart.

THE THREE STAGES OF FORGIVENESS

When I teach about forgiveness, I've found it helpful to describe the process in terms of three stages. Like RAIN, these are not invariable, but they provide a useful map.

THE THREE STAGES OF FORGIVENESS

Intending to forgive

Making the U-turn with RAIN

Including a Real Other in our heart

In my own practice, when I realize I am caught in the trance of blame, I ask myself three questions that help guide me through these three stages of awakening from blame:

- What is my deepest intention in this relationship? This reminds me of my longing for an awake, open heart—a forgiving heart.
- What am I unwilling to feel (or running from) inside me? This enables the U-turn, shifting my attention from the other person to the vulnerability under my armoring of blame.
- What is really true about this person? How might they be struggling? What matters most to them? This helps me remember the person's humanness, suffering, and goodness.

Stage 1 of Forgiveness: Intending to Forgive

I know many students who feel that to be on a spiritual path, they *should* be forgiving. They see anger and blame as embarrassing comments on their spiritual development. Yet forgiving is not something that an ego-self can dictate. In fact, self-judgment or shame makes forgiveness more difficult.

You can't will forgiveness, but you can be willing. This is an essential understanding. There is some wisdom, beyond your ego, that knows that for your heart to be free, it needs to be inclusive, not blaming. From this place, you understand that you can't truly be happy or feel loving if you are holding on to anger and blame. As the Zen teacher Charlotte Joko Beck writes, "Our incapacity to forgive is directly related to our inability to feel joy in our life."

This place of inner wisdom gives rise to the deep intention toward forgiving. You might feel it as a tender hope or prayer that your heart can relax and open, that you can experience the freedom of a fearless, forgiving heart. This intention to forgive carries real power. In the moments when your intention or prayer is sincere and deep, you become available for healing and transformation. Simply having the intention to forgive opens the door for the whole process of forgiving to unfold.

REFLECTION: INTENDING TO FORGIVE

As you've been reading, have you thought about a person you are pushing away with blame or resentment? Can you sense how the trance of blame keeps you small and rigid? How you are forgetting your own gold and theirs? You might call on your future self—the wisest, most loving place in you—and imagine just for a moment what it would be like to have the heartspace that includes this person. Can you sense the freedom that is possible?

Now bring this person to mind and mentally whisper, "My intention is to forgive you, [calling the person by name]." Can you feel the sincerity of your intention, even if some parts of you are still unready? Trust that with the mindfulness and compassion of RAIN, your heart will become increasingly inclusive, forgiving, and free.

Stage 2 of Forgiveness: Making the U-Turn with RAIN

Our intention to forgive motivates us to do the deep work of RAIN. Once we've set our intention, we'll more readily Recognize when we go into trance. We can then choose to pause and Allow the experience to come more fully into awareness.

We actively step on the path of forgiveness when we make the U-turn. We shift our attention from outwardly directed thoughts of blame so that we can directly Investigate our inner vulnerability. This is where we really face the hurts and fears that live under the armoring of blame. Healing begins here: With Nurturing, the last step of RAIN, we bring a tender presence to the parts inside us that most need our attention. This dissolves protective armoring and helps soothe, ease, and open our heart.

I'll return to Stefan to show how RAIN, and the U-turn, worked for him.

When Stefan signed up for our spring retreat, he hoped he'd find some relief from his anger toward his father. Being challenged by his sister had upped the ante. And his meditations were revealing how he was creating his own suffering. "I sit there running all these movies about how bad he is and drive myself crazy. Then I tell myself, 'I'm the one feeling this . . . he's just living his life.'" Stefan's intention to forgive was becoming increasingly conscious and strong.

Yet during the first few days of the retreat, his mind seemed, as he put it, "hell-bent on fueling the flames." "Every thought of him brings up anger," he told me when we met on the third day. "I see that condescending look, and it's like he's still in control . . . making me miserable." After a long pause, he continued, "And yet he's this old man shuffling around an efficiency apartment. I want to be forgiving—my sister's right. But I'm still so triggered."

"What you're feeling is natural," I said. "We usually can't just decide to drop anger and open our hearts, especially when there's a deep wound. If you want to truly forgive, the starting place is bringing your full attention to what you're actually feeling . . . and we can do this with RAIN."

It was quite easy for Stefan to Recognize and Allow his blaming thoughts, so I invited him to make the U-turn and Investigate.

"If you step out of the mental stories of blame, where do you feel the anger in your body?" I asked.

After a few moments, he responded, "Right here," and put both hands, one over the other, on the center of his chest.

I said, "Notice what the sensations of anger are like, and let them be as strong as they are. If it helps to keep your attention there, you might leave your hands where they are."

He nodded and his brows furrowed, his jaw clenched. Then, after some moments, he sighed, lowered his hands, and seemed to slump in his chair. I asked him what he was aware of.

"The anger got intense, and then it sort of collapsed. I feel deflated, defeated . . ." He was silent for a bit, then added in a soft voice, "I was a disappointment. I just wasn't male enough for him to respect me."

I encouraged Stefan to continue Investigating by sensing what happened in his body when he was believing that—that he wasn't male enough.

"There's hurt. It's this young part of me . . . in my chest . . . he's ashamed, he's lonely, he's crying . . . but silently."

"If he could speak, what would he say?"

"I will never have a father who sees me, who likes me, who wants me as his son." As he said these words out loud, Stefan put his face in his hands and began sobbing. This was the pain his anger and blame were covering, the deep grief of loss.

I waited a bit and, when he quieted, asked gently, "What does that part of you most need from you right now?"

"To know I'm here, that I care." I invited Stefan to Nurture that young part of himself by mentally sending that message several times, sincerely, really meaning it.

He again crossed his hands, placed them on his chest, and became very still. A few minutes later, he opened his eyes and said, "Thanks—something lifted a bit; there's more space, ease."

I encouraged Stefan to take all the time he needed with the U-turn. Later in the retreat, as I looked out at the students meditating, I often saw Stefan with two hands crossed on his chest. Then, during our last group meeting, Stefan stood up and shared his "takeaway" from the retreat: "I can make myself a victim by blaming someone else, or I can heal and empower myself." He put one hand on his chest for a moment and then added, "It's a choice."

The shift in identity out of victimhood is a gift experienced in After the RAIN. I often think of a line from a movie I saw many years ago: "Vengeance is a lazy form of grief." When I share this with others, they understand. Blaming others is easier than facing the reality of our hurts, fears, and losses. Yet it's only when we make the U-turn of RAIN, bringing a healing attention to our inner life, that we can access our full strength, wisdom, and compassion. The U-turn undoes victimhood and empowers us to see past the mask of Unreal Other. And this allows us to extend our compassion in ever-widening circles.

Stage 3 of Forgiveness: Including a Real Other in Our Heart

Imagine that you are walking in the woods and see a dog sitting by a tree. You go over to greet it, and suddenly it springs at you with bared fangs. You jump back, angry and afraid. Then you notice that one of its paws is caught in a trap. Your entire mood shifts, and now you are filled with concern. Still, you might not step too close; it's dangerous. But your heart actively wants to help this dog.

The shift from blame to care occurs the moment you realize that the dog's aggression is coming from vulnerability and pain. This applies to us all: When we behave in hurtful ways, it is because we are caught in some kind of painful trap.

You might bring to mind someone who has hurt you. Can you see how he or she is entrapped by wounds and fears? When Oprah Winfrey did a show about childhood trauma, she talked about how early wounds become precursors to violent behavior. Rather than blame, she said, a person needs to ask this important question: "What happened?" What pain from the past drove this behavior? In a *New York Times* interview, the rapper Jay-Z put it this way: "'Oh, you got bullied as a kid so you trying to bully me. I understand.' And once I understand that, instead of reacting to that with anger, I can provide a softer landing and maybe, 'Aw, man, is you O.K.?'"

If we could read the secret history of our enemies, we should find in each man's life sorrow and suffering enough to disarm all hostility.

• HENRY WADSWORTH LONGFELLOW

We won't be able to see a bully's vulnerability if they've just injured us. But we can see this secret suffering once we've taken care of ourselves.

When I saw Stefan after the retreat, he spoke differently about his father. "We had him to dinner, he was slouched in his chair, clearly getting tired, and my son said, 'Hey, Gramps, how about a game of ping pong?' My father immediately sat up tall, made up something about a show he was watching that he needed to get back to. He hated showing vulnerability."

Stefan was touched by his dad's pride and powerlessness, and seeing his "leg in a trap" softened and opened Stefan's heart. He started loosening up, and his father responded in kind. The two watched a Netflix series together, had competitions to see who made the best popcorn, and during the week would text about favorite teams (Patriots versus Steelers).

Six months later, his father had another, even more serious heart attack. At the hospital one evening, Stefan was reading the news aloud when his father put out his hand . . . a signal to stop. Then Stefan heard the words he had never expected to hear: "I know I wasn't the right dad for you, but I don't think you know how much I've always loved you." His father's eyes were wet, and the two held each other's gaze for some time. These were moments that Stefan, long after his father's passing some months later, would always remember.

When Stefan shared this with me, he said, "You know, Tara, I think what made it possible for him to say that was that he felt forgiven by me; it was safe enough."

I don't share this story as a promise that if you forgive someone, they will come around. But the truth is, the energy of our open heart affects others in profound ways, some seen and some unseen. And it frees us as well.

THE GIFT OF FORGIVENESS

Both giving and receiving forgiveness are pure expressions of radical compassion. Both evolve us. When we open in forgiveness, we reconnect with our own openheartedness. When we feel forgiven, we are able to trust our belonging and our basic goodness. Like breathing in and breathing out, giving and receiving are interrelated: Both allow us to remember and live from the gold.

The author Scott McClanahan tells of a man who left home after an ugly fight with his parents. He stayed away for many years, a few of which he spent in jail. Some months after he was released, he wrote to his parents saying he'd be coming home and giving the date. He said that if they wanted to see him and were not ashamed of what had happened and of where he wound up, they should put a blanket on the clothesline. On the appointed day when he got off the train, he became anxious and started having painful doubts that they'd want to see him. The doubts became more insistent as he got closer to home and remembered the horrible words that had been exchanged. He was about to turn back when he saw a blanket in a tree. Then he saw another. And as the house came into sight, he saw that the clothesline was covered in blankets, the yard was covered in blankets, the roof was covered in blankets. His parents were standing there, and they were welcoming him inside.

We long to be included in each other's hearts. And we long to love others without holding back. What could be more beautiful than dedicating ourselves to putting out blankets of forgiveness, letting those we've pushed away feel us welcoming them home?

PRACTICE: THE RAIN OF FORGIVENESS

Forgiving others has two essential phases: The first is an inner process of healing the woundedness beneath the blame, and the second is bringing a compassionate attention to the other person involved. Please consider the first part below as a "stand alone" meditation, and practice it as long as it takes (days, months, years) to feel well established in self-compassion. Then, when you are ready, practice them both as a sequence.

—⟐—

Sit in a comfortable way, closing your eyes and coming into stillness. Take several full breaths, and with each exhale, release any tension you are aware of. Begin by reflecting on your intention to cultivate a forgiving heart that includes yourself and all beings.

PART I: RAIN to the Wounds Beneath Blame

Scan your life, and sense where you might be feeling unforgiving toward someone and caught in anger and/or blame. Remind yourself of what happened (or is happening) to cause these feelings. You might ask yourself, "What is the worst part of this? What about this most upsets me?"

"What am I believing about this person? What am I believing about how they are relating to me?"

Recognize: Mentally note whatever feelings and thoughts are predominant as you bring this person to mind.

Allow: Pause and Allow this experience to be here, as it is, without any judgment or effort to do anything.

Investigate: Now make the U-turn, letting go of thoughts of the other person and bringing your full attention to what is happening inside you.

- Discover how your upset feelings and thoughts about the person express themselves as *feelings in your body:* Where are those feelings strongest? What are they like? Take your time to fully enter and feel the part of you that is most distressed.
- You might ask this hurting part the following: "How do you want me to be with you? What do you most need? Is it acceptance? Protection? Understanding? Forgiveness? Compassion? Love?"

Nurture: Call on your wisest, most loving self (your future self, your awakened heart). Imagine that you can listen and respond from your future self: How might you offer what is most needed? Is there a touch (like your hand on your heart), a message, or an image that helps that wounded part receive what it needs?

Take some moments (thirty seconds) to bring Nurturing to this part and to sense how this part experiences the compassion that is offered.

(Note: If it is difficult to access your own awakened heart, you can call on whatever source of loving feels most accessible—a friend or family member, a deity, your dog—to help Nurture the inner part.)

After the RAIN: Notice and rest in the sense of who you are when you are offering and receiving inner Nurturing.

PART II: RAIN of Forgiveness to Another

After completing part 1, bring your attention to the other person. Sense that you are viewing that person from the awareness of your future self—witnessing him or her with your wisest, most compassionate heart. (You might experiment and imagine that you are doing this reflection ten to fifteen years in the future.)

Recognize: Mentally note whatever you observe about the other person.

Allow: Pause and Allow this experience of the person to be there, just as it is.

Investigate: You might ask yourself this: "What is the vulnerability—the fears, hurts, unmet needs—that might drive this person to cause suffering? How does this person have a leg in a trap?"

Nurture: Offer forgiveness through the following phrases,

or through your own compassionate words and/or visual images: Mentally whispering the person's name and saying, "I see and feel the harm you have caused, and I forgive you now." Or, if you're not yet ready to forgive, "I see and feel the harm you have caused, and it is my intention to forgive you." Repeat several times.

If you do feel able to include this person in a forgiving heart, you might follow the forgiveness phrases with whatever caring wish resonates for the healing of this person's suffering.

After the RAIN: Notice the quality of heartspace that has arisen, and let it be as large and inclusive as it is. You might inquire, "Who am I when resting in a forgiving heart?"

With forgiveness practices, it is common to judge ourselves for how well or fully we are able to do the meditation. Let go of any judgments you are carrying, and honor the sincerity of your intention to open and free your heart. End the meditation by releasing all ideas of self and other. Simply rest in the experience of tender awareness. If a thought or feeling arises, sense the capacity to include this entire living dying world in the vast space of a forgiving heart.

QUESTIONS AND RESPONSES

My partner grew up with a rageful, narcissistic mother who lashed out at her almost daily. Now she's doing the same with our teenage daughters. I understand that her painful past is probably behind this behavior. But she's an adult now. Shouldn't she take responsibility for the harm she's causing?

When we've caused harm, true healing requires taking responsibility for our behavior, asking for forgiveness when possible, and making amends. Being able to acknowledge honestly the hurt we've caused is actually empowering and reduces self-blame.

Yet, just as wounds from our past can drive us to hurt ourselves and others, they also make it difficult to change our behavior. Prolonged emotional abuse in childhood is known to undermine the development of capacities like executive functioning, self-regulation, mindfulness, and empathy—all crucial to becoming a fully responsible adult. For someone like your partner, admitting that she is causing harm can feel dangerous, bringing up intolerable emotions of shame and fear of rejection.

As you struggle with this situation, you may find it helpful to consider the word "should" as a flag. It tells you that your beliefs about good or right behavior, no matter how logical and reasonable they may be, are at odds with the reality of how your partner is right now. And crucially, when someone's acting from unprocessed wounds, blaming doesn't help. Blame punishes: It reinforces the core wound of "Something is wrong with me." As you might have experienced with your partner, it also evokes defensiveness and/or denial. Rather than serving positive change, it perpetuates the hurtful behavior.

Of course, you need to communicate clearly that your partner can't go on hurting your daughters and to create boundaries that will protect them. As a co-parent, this is critical—otherwise you are enabling harmful behavior. But it is possible to communicate and seek the way to change from a place of care rather than blame. Just as with children, the wounded inner child of adults needs nurturing to grow and change. I've never seen anyone evolve and stop behaving hurtfully in response to "shoulds," anger, or blame. All research shows that punishment doesn't work for genuine healing and transformation but that care and rehabilitation do.

Yet shifting from "should" and blame to compassion for your partner is possible only if you take good care of the parts within yourself that, quite naturally, might be feeling powerless, angry, bitter, self-righteous, hurt, and afraid. You are being called to inhabit your highest self, for the sake of yourself, your partner, and your children. You might need help from a therapist to create a safe, compassionate space for communicating as both you and your partner move toward becoming allies and together move toward transformation and healing.

Some people believe that people are doing the best that they can. Do you think this is true?

If you scan your own life, you'll see times when you're relating to people with presence and care and other times when you're preoccupied, reactive, even hurtful. Yet if you focus on a particular situation you deeply regret and ask, "What stopped me from being more sensitive, kind, accepting, aware . . . ?" you'll probably realize that you were in trance—below the line—with your attention narrowed. Your thoughts and behavior were driven by deeply grooved habits of distractedness, by emotions like anxiety or aversion, or by cravings for pleasure or relief from distress. Your survival brain was in charge, and you were cut off from your more recently evolved prefrontal cortex. Your brain was doing the best it could, calling on its primitive coping strategies and trying to satisfy unmet needs.

The mindfulness and compassion of RAIN cultivate an integrated brain. This means that even when we're emotionally triggered, rather than suffer a full limbic hijack, we have some awareness of what's happening and increased access to our inner resources. We have more choice to live from our full potential, our true "best."

Getting angry and blaming my partner for the ways he hurts me is the only way to get his attention. For me, forgiving him would mean living with abuse.

Anger, blame, and punishment can work to temporarily control another's behavior. The question is, Does that really change the behavior and give us the relationship we want?

A woman taking my weekly class told me that her husband physically bullied her throughout their four years of marriage. As she put it, "I flip-flopped back and forth from a hurt, scared victim to an angry victim." When she'd explode in rage and threaten to leave, her husband would grovel. He'd swear the assaults would end and beg for her forgiveness and another chance.

She'd agree to stay, each time hoping that this time he'd really be different.

As she practiced the U-turn of RAIN, dropping blaming thoughts and attending to her inner experience, she finally came face-to-face with the truth of her suffering—"This is the suffering of abuse." And she knew that Nurture meant she had to take care of herself. Shifting away from anger and blame enabled her to Recognize and accept reality: She was suffering, he wasn't going to change, and she could do something about her situation. She moved to her sister's house and filed for divorce. Real forgiveness came, but it took a long time, even after she felt safe.

Anger is a signal. It energizes us to take care. But if we want to step out of being a disempowered, angry victim, we need to move on from blame. This is true whether our partner is abusive, our teen steals money from us, or a sibling manipulates a shared inheritance. If we can let go of the aversive energy of blame, we gain access to the wisdom we need to respond effectively to our situation.

NINE

Seeing the Goodness

*To love someone is to learn the song in their heart
and sing it to them when they have forgotten.*

• ARNE GARBORG

*It is a sobering thought that the finest act of love you
can perform is not an act of service but an act of
contemplation, of seeing. When you serve people,
you help, support, comfort, alleviate pain. When you
see them in their inner beauty and goodness, you
transform and create.*

• ANTHONY DE MELLO

The couple had asked to meet with me after one of our Wednesday night classes, and even before they spoke, I could see the worry in their faces. It was about Jono, they said, their twenty-three-year-old son.

Jono had learning disabilities, and he'd dropped out after two years at a small liberal arts college. Since then, he'd been living at home and working part-time at Home Depot to contribute to the household. "I tried to get him to take courses at a community college," his father told me, "but no way. Then I tried to get him to do career counseling, and he refused that too. He's hanging out with old high school friends—nice kids, but they're not going anywhere." He added grimly, "It seems like all Jono wants is to watch movies, go mountain biking, or mess around with his video camera . . . certainly not the makings of a secure future."

At this point, Jono's mom jumped in. "It's not that we don't like having him around . . . we do, we adore him! He's a sweetheart—but lately he mopes around and barely talks to us—he's not his old self."

I could feel how deeply they cared about Jono and told them so. The mom's eyes filled with tears. "Oh, we do, we do. And we're so afraid for his future." Then she looked at me imploringly. "But what should we do?" she asked. "Should I pray for him and surround him with white light? Should we bring him here and urge him to meditate? We'd do anything to help him."

"I do have a suggestion," I said, "but first, let me ask you both a question." They leaned in, curious. "What are the qualities that you really love and appreciate about Jono?"

"Oh," said his mom without hesitation, "he's always been the kindest person you've ever met . . . so sensitive to others' feelings. And he can be great fun to be around; he's got a wacky sense of humor."

His dad added, "And I'll admit Jono's a creative guy. . . . I'm impressed with what he can do with that camera." Then he added thoughtfully, "He's really smart. He just hasn't found a way to apply his intelligence that translates."

"Whoa," I said, and then smiled. "That's for another time. For right now, thank you! You're bringing Jono to life for me."

I went on to suggest that each day during their meditation they reflect on what they most loved and respected about their son. "Let yourself feel your appreciation for who he is deep in your body, in your heart. And then when you're with him, just notice how he's doing—his mood, energy, that kind of thing. Stay with that for a couple of months, and then let's meet again."

When we did, both of them seemed calmer. This time, Jono's mom went first: "Maybe that practice you gave us just relaxes me, but the more I remember Jono's strengths, the more I feel like everything will work out."

Her husband nodded. "At first I thought you were just telling us to let go, but it was a lot more than that. . . . We still don't know how he'll find his way; we're just more sure he will."

Before they left, I shared something I'd found with my own son: The more I trusted in him doing well, the better he did. My confidence was contagious.

I met with Jono's parents for the last time a few months later. They reported that he had been volunteering as a video editor at a local nonprofit and that he was planning to return to school for a degree in digital video production. Most important, he seemed more like his old self; on Father's Day, he'd presented his dad with a "news spot" he'd made announcing his promotion to CEO of Home Depot. Jono had regained his sparkle and playfulness, and he was finding his way.

Our relationships, especially the close ones, easily lock into rigid patterns of communication that block true intimacy and healing. The mindfulness and nurturing of RAIN can release us from the grip of these persistent habits. While I didn't review the formal practice of RAIN with Jono's parents, you can see the steps unfolding in how they related to him: They

Recognized that he was having a hard time and that they were distressed; rather than continuing to react, they paused and Allowed him to be as he was; they Investigated by shifting their attention from what was wrong to what they trusted about him—his goodness; and they laid the grounds of Nurturing by filling themselves with genuine appreciation for him. Through this informal practice of RAIN, they stepped out of fear-based reactivity and became able to offer Jono what he most needed: trust in who he was.

WHAT IS BASIC GOODNESS?

For Jono and his parents, healing emerged when they shifted their attention from what was wrong to remembering what I call "basic goodness."

What does this mean? If you recall the image of the Golden Buddha in chapter 3, you might think of our day-to-day social self or personality as the protective clay coverings. These coverings—our appearance, manners, defenses, judgments, skills, weaknesses, and so on—are often evaluated in terms of "good self" and "bad self." The good self meets the standards we have adopted from our caregivers, peers, and the larger society. Perhaps our good self is polite, hardworking, attractive, and accomplished. Our bad self is all the ways we fall short—when we call ourselves selfish, impatient, judgmental, or impulsive.

But none of these conditioned ego patterns limit or express our basic goodness. Basic goodness is the gold of our true nature: the universal qualities of awareness, aliveness, love, creativity, and intelligence that live through all of us. Our changing moods, behaviors, and personalities are like surface waves. Basic goodness is the ocean itself. If we remain focused on our conditioned patterns, if we judge or identify with these patterns, we can easily miss our vastness and depth.

Because fear constricts the expression of basic goodness, it's easiest to recognize the gold in others when they are relaxed and present. We often see it shining in children before their personalities have taken shape. One friend told me about gazing at a picture of her nine-month-old granddaughter, filled with wonder at the pure sentience and brightness in her eyes. Suddenly she recalled a long-forgotten line of poetry: "There lives the dearest freshness deep down things."

SEEING THE GOODNESS

Because we all have different bodies, minds, and personalities, the gold lives through our evolving beings in myriad ways.

I asked my social media friends to share examples of seeing basic goodness in others. Here is how some of them finished the sentence "I see the goodness . . .":

- on my husband's face when he sees the kids after an out-of-town trip.
- when my youngest son hears the fatigue in my voice and brings me a cup of water.
- in my wife when she greets the parking attendant or cashier with such kindness, attention, and respect.
- when my best friend hugs his dog with deep affection.
- in my five-year-old daughter, who says to the sun at sunset, 'Good-bye, I love you.'

- when my husband pulls over to help someone whose car has died—and never takes anything for his time.
- when my partner is tender and willing to stay in the relationship to work out our difficulties.
- when my dad was disabled after a massive stroke, and he still would ask me, 'Sweetheart, can I get you anything?'

Shortly after I posted this inquiry, I received a birthday card from a dear friend. Her message began, "I see your basic goodness when . . ." As I read her words, my eyes filled with tears; I felt so deeply loved and seen. And then I was flooded by a sense of *her* basic goodness—the gold shining forth, the beauty of her deep and loving attention. I was reminded of one of my favorite quotations, by Thomas Merton:

Then it was as if I suddenly saw the secret beauty of their hearts, the depths of their hearts where neither sin nor desire nor self-knowledge can reach, the core of their reality, the person that each one is in God's eyes. If only they could all see themselves as they really *are*. If only we could see each other that way all the time. There would be no more war, no more hatred, no more cruelty, no more greed. . . . I suppose the big problem would be that we would fall down and worship each other.

MIRRORING TELLS US WHO WE ARE

The author Alice Walker tells this story:

> In the Babemba tribe of South Africa, when a person acts irresponsibly or unjustly, he is placed in the center of the village, alone and unfettered.
>
> All work ceases, and every man, woman and child in the village gathers in a large circle around the accused individual. Then each person in the tribe speaks to the accused, one at a time, about all the good things the person in the center of the circle has done in his lifetime. Every incident, every experience that can be recalled with any detail and accuracy is recounted. All his positive attributes, good deeds, strengths and kindnesses are recited carefully and at length.
>
> The tribal ceremony often lasts several days. At the end, the tribal circle is broken, a joyous celebration takes place, and the person is symbolically and literally welcomed back into the tribe.

Our trust in our own basic goodness emerges from the clear and deep mirroring of others. The nurture we need to survive as infants comes not only from warm milk, not only from the warmth of being held and comforted, but also from the loving energy of a caregiver's gaze. When we feel seen and heard and responded to with care, the message is "You matter. You are part of us. You belong and are loved." When our growing curiosity and playfulness are met with delight, the message is

"Your aliveness and unfolding are valued; all of what you are is welcome in this world."

Mirroring the gold in our children (and each other) requires basic elements of radical compassion: clarity, openhearted presence, and emotional intelligence. But when we're "below the line"—in trance—we quickly fixate on the "coverings" of a child's behavior and then react with impatience, judgment, or anger or withdraw into disinterest or preoccupation. This reactivity can feed a sense of our own deficiency as parents and drive us even more below the line. And if reactive trance becomes habitual, the child easily internalizes the bad-self message: "Something is wrong with me."

Most of us give and receive a mix of clear and distorted mirroring. When I think back to my son's youth, what jumps out now is that I always had something to worry about! In grade school, I worried that he didn't have many friends. In middle school, he was "too social"—always wanting to hang out. In high school, it was video gaming, partying, procrastination, lack of academic focus. And my worrying went hand in hand with judgment, controlling, and the message "You should be different." Behind all this was the trance of unworthiness and fear: "I'm failing as a mother. This is my fault. If I don't fix it, he might not have a good life."

But he always had my love and appreciation as well, and he must have sensed how my heart lit up as I watched him delight in Rollerblading or return inspired from a wilderness vision quest, when I learned how he had consoled a friend in trouble or marveled at his mastery of Magic: The Gathering. When I see him now as a young therapist and entrepreneur, husband

and father, I know that the times when I beamed out genuine appreciation and trust in his unfolding were the times that most served his confidence and well-being.

CAN WE OVERDO POSITIVE MIRRORING?

Our strengths and talents—the parts we might call the "good self"—are real parts of us! And when they're recognized—especially when we doubt ourselves or lack confidence—it can be a real gift. But some praise is not healthy mirroring. Maybe you were constantly affirmed and rewarded for good grades, for being attractive, cooperative, artistic, or athletic. What was the message you absorbed? For many of us, it was "This is what I have to do to be lovable and good, and I can't slip up." And along with that belief came a chronic fear of falling short, of making a mistake, of not being the best, of risking something new. Trying to pump up someone's self-esteem with excessive praise polishes the covering over the Golden Buddha, but it distances them from the gold.

WHAT ABOUT MIRRORING WEAKNESS OR VULNERABILITY?

Mirroring a person's weaknesses (or what they experience as "bad self") will be helpful only if you have first established your caring and respect for them and belief in their basic goodness. Otherwise, they are likely to be too hurt or defensive to even take in your message. Most of us know what it's like to receive criticism when we don't feel appreciated in a fundamental way. Our entire being gets armored in reactivity!

But when trust and caring are there, our mirroring can help others Recognize unconscious behaviors, emotions, or beliefs that are creating suffering and separation. Parents serve their children by letting them know how their rudeness or deceit, carelessness or anger, impacts others. Therapists mirror unprocessed emotions like fear or shame, helping their clients bring them into awareness. A trusted friend or colleague might mirror our sense of loss and sorrow, helping us feel accompanied and seen.

Clear and deep mirroring can bring radical healing at any age. During my Ph.D. internship, I had a psychotherapy supervisor who had the gift of what he called "seeing the beloved." Rob offered his full presence to his clients, and he reflected their goodness in ways they could hear and trust. He found the courage in their vulnerability, the dedication in their honesty, the depth of their longing to heal or awaken. They'd leave their sessions more at home in themselves, increasingly attuned to the gold. And he did the same with us, his students.

I remember how, in one of our weekly supervision groups, Rob picked up on my worry. I was very fond of a client, but I'd become concerned that I lacked the skill necessary to work with her. "You really care about her, don't you?" he said, nodding with his affectionate smile. Then, looking around, he addressed us all. "Don't ever underestimate the power of it . . . your pure caring. I can't tell you what technique is better than what, but caring . . . that's the magic ingredient." His words cleared the worry from my heart, and something more. They showed me how simple the gift of mirroring can be.

I could not lie anymore,
so I started to call my dog "God."
First he looked confused,
then he started smiling, then he even danced.
I kept at it: now he doesn't even bite.
I am wondering if this might work on people?

● SANT TUKARAM, *seventeenth-century poet-saint,*
translated by Daniel Ladinsky

SEEING OUR OWN GOODNESS: SELF-NURTURING WITH RAIN

Recall a time when you were really down on yourself. When you were in the thick of it, did you have even an inkling of your own good heart, of your care for others, of your growing capacity for honesty and presence? How much were you seeing the goodness in your family, friends, or colleagues?

When we're trapped in self-judgment, our perceptual filter narrows and our mirroring becomes distorted. We monitor ourselves to see how we're falling short, become preoccupied with hiding our inadequacy, and stay busy justifying, proving, or improving ourselves. And this self-mistrust inevitably extends to others.

When feelings of self-aversion or unworthiness are strong, the full practice of RAIN (see RAIN Step-by-Step in chapter 3) helps us bring mindfulness and self-compassion to the limiting beliefs and feelings that are covering over the gold. As we Investigate, we contact the deep vulnerability that is driving us and, by Nurturing, reconnect with a larger, more loving presence.

We can also directly call on the Nurturing step of RAIN at any time, by intentionally looking for and reflecting on the goodness within us, as in the Reflection below.

REFLECTION: RECALLING YOUR GOODNESS AT DIFFICULT TIMES

When we are caught in the trance of unworthiness, it can be hard to believe in our own goodness. Bring yourself into presence in whatever way works best for you, and then try one or more of the following prompts.

- Recall someone—a person, a spiritual figure, a pet— for whom you can easily feel appreciation and love. Sense the goodness of your care for this being.
- Recall a time when you were kind or generous.
- Reflect on qualities you appreciate in yourself (such as your love of nature, adventurousness, humor, curiosity, persistence).
- Imagine yourself as a child, and then recall any moment of playfulness, affection, or wonder that stands out for you.
- Bring to mind someone you trust, someone who appreciates and loves you, and try to look at yourself through their eyes.
- Imagine your future self, the self who expresses your deepest intention and potential, the self you are growing into.

I often refer to RAIN, and especially to the practice of Nurturing, as spiritual re-parenting. We are learning to offer ourselves the kind of mirroring that we all needed as young children. As you experiment with these different reflections, see what works for you. (Just as there are many styles of good parenting, there are many different approaches to spiritual nurturing.) You are undoing the fears and self-doubt that come from years of distorted mirroring, and it takes many rounds. With each round, spend time in After the RAIN, sensing who you are when you feel Nurturing and Nurtured. The more often you get any taste of your basic goodness, the easier it becomes in daily life to reconnect with the gold.

BECOMING A MIRROR OF GOODNESS FOR OTHERS

Nelson Mandela wrote, "It never hurts to think too highly of a person; often they become ennobled and act better because of it."

Can you remember times of positive mirroring that made a difference to you? I still recall moments that deepened my confidence in life-changing ways. There was the parent of a friend who told me that I had a special way of listening that could help others. There was the Harvard Divinity student, a friend's older brother, who responded to my probing philosophical questions by telling me I was "spiritually deep." And when I first became serious about yoga, my yoga teacher told me one day that she could sense my dedication to the path. These few words helped me Recognize and trust my own being. They became companions on my journey, and remembering their impact still inspires me to offer the gift of mirroring to others.

REFLECTION: BENEFACTORS WHO HAVE NURTURED YOU

Sitting comfortably, close your eyes and relax your body. Now, looking back through your life, bring to mind a person who had a positive influence on you. Ask yourself, "When did they mirror something about me that helped me trust my goodness?" As a memory arises, pause and allow yourself to appreciate them, and feel how their words or actions Nurtured you.

Becoming a mirror of goodness is a deliberate training in radical compassion. When we're in trance—preoccupied, anxious, reactive, on autopilot—we're often blind to the goodness of others. Instead, we fixate on what we don't like, what seems wrong. If we want to become clear and nurturing mirrors to others, we need first to be conscious, present, and intentional.

LOOKING TO SEE GOODNESS: THREE KEY QUESTIONS

- What does this person care about?
- Am I looking with fresh eyes?
- What is the best way to let them know their goodness?

What Does This Person Care About?

Logan, a young man who had attended a number of our retreats, was consistently harsh with himself and filled with self-
doubt. During one of our meetings, I asked him if he could
recall any recent moments of respite, times when he felt at home
with himself. Yes, there had been one the day before, he said.
During a meditation, he'd noticed an elderly woman who was
sitting on a chair across the room. Her feet were dangling because they couldn't reach the floor, and this looked so uncomfortable that he got up and found a cushion to put under them.
When he returned to his place, he'd become aware of a sense of
inner warmth, connectedness, and peace.

I paused a minute and said, "Logan, that was such a caring
thing to do. . . . I really get that kindness matters to you, and
that you live it." As we continued to talk, I told him I was confident that he had a lot to offer others and that he had the makings of a fine meditation teacher. Before we ended, I thanked
him for being so sweet to the older woman—who, as it happened, was my mother! We parted with tears, both touched by
our shared reflection on kindness.

Two years later, Logan was teaching meditation in prisons
and also working with teens. In an email, he told me about a
seventeen-year-old girl who seemed trapped in unrelenting
self-criticism. During a teen retreat he was co-teaching, he'd
asked if she could remember a time when her mind was at ease,
and she told him about helping someone in their meditation
group. As I had done with him, he mirrored her kindness and
goodness back to her. And when he asked how she'd felt while

she was helping the other teen, her face softened. "I felt like there was nothing wrong with me," she said.

You can clearly see a person's goodness when they are doing what they love. This is when you can sense what most matters to them, what brings them fully alive. Reminding them of this goodness can help someone undo a lifetime of self-aversion or alienation. When we ask ourselves, "What does this person care about most deeply?" we become able to see past the surface wants and fears—the ego coverings—and help them to do the same.

Am I Looking with Fresh Eyes?

Often we deprive those closest to us of our mirroring because we see them through the eyes of habit. We are in trance, caught in our assumptions about what they are like and how they think and feel. In the words of the poet T. S. Eliot,

> What we know of other people
> Is only our memory of the moments
> During which we knew them. And they have changed
>   since then.
> We must also remember
> That at every meeting we are meeting a stranger.

In order to get past familiarity, we need to train ourselves to see afresh, to become genuinely curious. One trick that works for me is to start by looking into someone's eyes and really wonder what color they are. And then extend that wondering to who is looking through those eyes. Do I know what they care about most right now? If I were seeing them for the first or last time, what is the quality of presence and care I'd most want to offer? If they were gone, what about their basic goodness would I remember?

Sometimes I'll choose one person, as Jono's parents did with him, and for some weeks make it a practice to see how their basic goodness is living through them.

> Look for things in them that you might have missed because of familiarity, for familiarity breeds staleness, blindness, and boredom. You cannot love what you cannot see afresh. You cannot love what you are not constantly discovering anew.
>
> • ANTHONY DE MELLO

What Is the Best Way to Let Them Know Their Goodness?

Expressing our appreciation is an intimate offering, and we might feel shy or uncomfortable, or fear that our comments won't be welcome. Maybe we think we aren't a significant figure in the other person's life and that what we are noticing won't really matter. Or perhaps it's simply not our habit.

The author and physician Rachel Naomi Remen tells a story about her grandfather, a rabbi, who called her *Neshume-le*, which means "little beloved soul." His words felt like blessings as they gave her great comfort and trust in her place in the world. After he died, Rachel told her mother how much these blessings had meant to her. Her mother responded, "Rachel,

I've blessed you every day of your life. I just never had the wisdom to do it out loud."

I've found that inner training, such as purposefully reflecting on goodness, warms us up to express our appreciation more naturally. This is why I had Jono's parents reflect on his goodness—to alter the focus of their attention.

In Buddhism, the loving-kindness (*metta*) meditation does just this. In the traditional meditation, we reflect on the goodness of a widening circle of beings—eventually including all life everywhere—and reflect on set phrases of well-wishing. Over the last several decades, I've found that this meditation becomes increasingly embodied and powerful when we experiment with visual imagery, touch, and whispering words. As I've mentioned, students have found it life changing to offer themselves loving kindness by gently placing a hand on their heart and whispering, "It's okay, sweetheart," or "This belongs," or "May you be happy," or whatever message most comforts.

My own experimenting led me to a practice that I continue to this day. During supper one evening toward the end of a monthlong silent retreat, I was touched by the gentleness and kindliness that emanated from an elderly man sitting nearby. I suddenly imagined that I was standing in front of him and we were looking into each other's eyes; then he closed his eyes, and I kissed him lightly on the brow. That image brought an upwelling of tenderness, a sense of soul connection. Since then, I've done this practice for dear ones, for people I don't know, and for those I've never met. I pause to see their goodness and then imagine offering some gesture of care—a kiss on the brow or sometimes a soft touch on their face or a gentle hug. Often I'll include a phrase of well-wishing, sometimes silent, sometimes whispered. This full, embodied practice opens me to a warm, tender heartspace—a field of communion that includes myself, whomever I've been reflecting on, and really all beings.

This meditation also reminds me to offer my blessings out loud. When I'm with a person I've been reflecting on, there's a more immediate sense of intimacy. I'm more inclined to Recognize their basic goodness and then ask myself, "How might I let them know?"

REFLECTION: A WARM-UP TO "SAYING IT OUT LOUD"

Take a few minutes to sit still, relax your body, and quiet your mind. When you feel present, bring to mind someone dear to you. Remind yourself of what you appreciate and love about them— perhaps the affectionate look in their eyes, their brightness, humor, honesty. Feel the warmth of your appreciation in your body.

—⊖—

Now imagine being with them in person and telling them some of the specific ways you experience their goodness. How do they receive your mirroring? How do you feel, having offered it? How does this sharing affect your feelings of connection?

End by taking some moments to renew your intention to offer the gift of mirroring in person.

TEN WAYS TO BRING LOVING-KINDNESS PRACTICE ALIVE IN YOUR DAILY LIFE

- Set an intention to reflect, each morning for a week, on the goodness of the people you live with or see most regularly. Then, whenever you remember to during the day, silently offer them your prayers.

- Whenever someone you know triggers feelings of irritation or insecurity, pause, recall some specific example of that person's goodness, and mentally whisper, "May you be happy."

- Choose a "neutral" person you encounter regularly, and whenever you see them during the following week, remind yourself of their goodness, and silently offer your wishes for their well-being. Notice if your feelings for this person change.

- Choose a "difficult" person, and set a time to reflect daily on his or her goodness. After you've offered prayers of loving kindness for at least two weeks, ask yourself, "Is there a change in my feelings? Has there been any change in their behavior toward me?"

- Discover what happens when you let someone know the goodness you are seeing in them.

- Keep your practice fresh and alive by experimenting with whatever words, images, or gestures awaken a genuine sense of connectedness and care.

- Explore whispering your prayer for yourself or another person aloud.

- Explore saying the name of the person you're praying for.
- Imagine and feel your heart holding the people you're praying for.
- Visualize them feeling healed and loved and uplifted by your prayer.

Even a few moments of reflecting on goodness and offering loving kindness can reconnect you with the purity of your loving heart.

TRANSCENDING BIAS: SEEING GOODNESS IN ALL BEINGS

Can you imagine moving through your day, appreciating the hearts and spirits of those you engage with, the beauty of clouds, birds, grasses, and trees? Of course you also include what's painful, perhaps your anger toward someone who's hurt you, or the suffering of a friend whose partner has Alzheimer's. Yet still, there's an awareness that remembers the goodness that animates our beings. Thomas Merton wrote, "Life is this simple: we are living in a world that is absolutely transparent and the divine is shining through it all the time. This is not just a nice story or a fable, it is true."

I heard a story read at a Christmas Eve church service that really brought this home.

One Christmas Day, a woman, her husband, and their

year-old son had driven a long way before they found an open diner by the side of the road.

It was quiet and almost empty, and they were waiting gratefully for their food when the little boy began waving from his high chair and calling, "Hi there!" to someone behind them. To the mother's dismay, it turned out to be a wreck of a man, unkempt and unwashed, obviously a homeless drunk. Now he was waving back at her boy and calling, "Hi there, baby, hi there, big boy . . . I see ya, buster."

The woman and her husband exchanged looks, and the few other people in the diner were shooting disapproving glances their way. And the old guy went on, even after their food came. "Do you know patty-cake? Attaboy . . . Do you know peekaboo? Hey, look, he knows peekaboo." The mother tried turning the high chair around, but her son shrieked and twisted to face his new buddy.

Finally, giving up on their meal, her husband got up to pay the bill, and the mother took the baby in her arms, praying that she could quickly get past the old drunk, who was seated by the door. But as they approached, her son reached out with both arms—his pick-me-up signal—and propelled himself into the man's open arms.

But now the mother could see tears in the man's eyes as her son laid his head on his shoulder. He gently held and rocked the boy, and then he looked straight into her eyes. "You take care of this baby," he said firmly. And as he slowly handed him back, "God bless you, ma'am. You've given me my Christmas gift."

She must have mumbled something in return, but as she rushed to the car, tears streaming down her face, she could only think, "My God, my God, forgive me."

Hearing this story, I felt a deep, aching remorse for the countless beings I had not seen. Learning to recognize what Merton calls the "secret beauty" is an evolutionary task for all of us: It is the very spirit of radical compassion. We need to spiritually re-parent ourselves and, by seeing the goodness in others, help them to trust who they are.

Yet as I will explain fully in the next chapter, we are conditioned to limit our attentiveness to a select few and, in a flash, unconsciously diminish many. Extending our conscious caring beyond those in our most immediate circle of family and friends is necessary for healing ourselves and our world.

MEDITATION: SEEING THE SECRET BEAUTY (LOVING KINDNESS)

The Buddhist metta (loving-kindness meditation), awakens our capacity for unconditional friendliness and love. Our hearts open as we bring our attention to the innate goodness within ourselves and all beings.

—⊖—

Sit in a way that allows you to be comfortable and relaxed. Letting go of whatever tension you can, loosen your shoulders, soften your hands, and relax your belly. Feel a smile spread through your eyes, softening the flesh around them. Bring a slight smile to your lips, and then feel the smile on the inside of your mouth. Smile into your heart, and then imagine the smile expanding, creating a receptive, tender space through the whole heart and chest area.

Now bring into your heart someone you love, ideally a

relationship that is not complicated. Take some moments to reflect on the qualities in this person you most appreciate. Recall their intelligence, humor, kindness, vitality. Picture this person when they are feeling love for you. Be aware of their essence as good and wakeful and caring. Mentally whisper their name and the words "thank you," and notice how your appreciation for this person fills your heart. Take a few moments to communicate your love by mentally whispering whatever prayer or phrase(s) of well-wishing most resonates for you. You might also imagine offering them an active gesture of love (kissing them on the brow, touching their cheek, hugging them).

Next, bring your attention to your own being and to the care in your heart. Take some moments to reflect on your own goodness—this caring for another and any other qualities that come to mind. Sense your deep aspiration—toward loving well, toward truth, toward living fully—and the goodness of your heart's intention.

If it's difficult to connect with your own goodness, bring to mind someone you trust who loves you, and look through their eyes. See who's here under the surface conditioning, the being you are evolving into (your future or true self). As you see your own goodness, you might also offer yourself a tender gesture of love, such as placing a hand lightly on your heart, and mentally whisper some words of care.

Now widen your circle of caring by bringing to mind a "neutral" person. (This might be someone you see regularly but don't know well or feel strongly about.) Take some moments to recall how this person looks, moves, and speaks. Now try to imagine them gazing at a beloved child . . . or struck by the beauty of a fresh snowfall . . . or laughing, relaxed, and at ease. Remind yourself that they want to be happy and don't want to suffer. Then, as this person comes alive for you, imagine offering them an active gesture of care and your prayer for their well-being.

Now bring to mind someone with whom you have a difficult relationship—perhaps someone who evokes anger, fear, or hurt. First take a moment to bring a kind, non-judging attention to your own feelings as you reflect on them. Then, turning back to this difficult person, try to see past the surface covering. Look to see some aspect of their basic goodness. It may help to imagine this person as a young child, sleeping peacefully—or at the other end of life, as someone who has just passed away. Can you recall something about them that you admire, some quality of dedication, caring, or creativity? Even if it's difficult to recognize this person's goodness, remind yourself that all humans want to be happy, want to avoid suffering. Remember that life matters to this person just as it does to you. Holding them in a gentle attention, imagine offering them a gesture of care and/or your prayer.

Next imagine that you are bringing together all those you have just prayed for—a dear person, yourself, a neutral one, a difficult one. Holding yourself and these others in your heart, sense your shared humanity, your vulnerability and basic goodness. Send prayers of care to all at once, recognizing that you are in this together.

Finally, allow your awareness to open out in all directions—in front of you, to either side, behind you, below you, and above you. In this vast space, sense that your loving presence is holding all beings: the wild creatures that fly and swim and run across fields; the dogs and cats that live in our homes; the life-forms that are threatened with extinction; the trees and grasses and flowers; children everywhere; humans living in great poverty and those with great riches; those at war and those at peace; those who are dying and those who are newly born. Imagine that you can hold the earth, our mother, in your lap and include all life everywhere in your boundless heart. Aware of the goodness inherent in all living beings, again offer your prayers.

After the RAIN: You might inquire, "Who am I when I'm sending out loving wishes?" Allow yourself to rest in openness and silence, letting whatever arises in your heart and awareness be touched by loving kindness.

QUESTIONS AND RESPONSES

How could everyone have secret beauty? What about Stalin, Hitler, Idi Amin? Aren't some people just evil?

The more we learn about the multiple factors that affect the formation of character—genetics, intergenerational trauma, abuse in childhood, social oppression, war—the more difficult it is to write off another human being as evil. As the Russian writer Aleksandr Solzhenitsyn, who spent years in labor camps under the Soviets, wrote,

> If only it were all so simple! If only there were evil people somewhere insidiously committing evil deeds, and it were necessary only to separate them from the rest of us and destroy them. But the line dividing good and evil cuts through the heart of every human being. And who is willing to destroy a piece of his own heart?

Yes, the human psyche is sometimes so deranged or wounded that most evidence of goodness is covered over. But if we remember that these "bad" people were once helpless children; if we imagine them weeping with sorrow, desperate for kindness or attention; if we know they don't want to suffer—perhaps then we can intuit some universal currents of goodness within them.

I often recall the words of a Tibetan teacher: "The essence of human bravery is refusing to give up on anyone." Assuming basic goodness helps us accept our own imperfections along with the flaws of others. No matter how buried in hatred, anger, or addiction someone may seem, goodness and the potential to awaken to it are always here. Trusting the gold is an intrinsic part of calling it forth.

What if letting someone know their goodness just swells their ego and blinds them to their weaknesses?

This question takes us back to the difference between a person's "good self" (the ego qualities that win us social acceptance) and the meaning of "basic goodness." Moderate praise of the "good self"—such as appreciating someone's athleticism, wit, physical beauty, or mathematical ability—may be affirming and even motivating in the short run. But as you suggest, excessive praise can cause unwholesome inflation. More important, it sends a stress-evoking message: We have to continuously *earn* the appreciation and love of others.

In contrast, when we mirror people's basic goodness, we are recognizing the universal qualities of love and awareness as they are expressed through them. We are mirroring the truth of who they are beyond any changing capacities. Far from inflating their ego, this message enables them to feel their belonging to life and gives them the peace that comes with being a part of the whole.

If you think of your own life, you can sense this difference. Over many years, I've found that no matter what my "good self" achieves, it does not relieve the trance of unworthiness. Yet whenever I remember basic goodness—when I feel loving connection, presence, awe, or gratitude—self-worth is no longer an issue. I'm at home in my true self.

You might think of your true self as an ocean that has changing waves on the surface. If you know you're the ocean, you're not afraid of the waves. (And if you forget you're the ocean, you'll be seasick every day.) Helping people see their basic goodness—their oceanness—does not blind them to the ego waves on the surface that need attention. To the contrary, as I've seen again and again, when we become confident of our basic goodness, we become increasingly dedicated to bringing the mindfulness and compassion of RAIN to whatever causes pain and separation.

TEN

The RAIN of Compassion

*Your path is not to seek for love but merely to seek
and find all the barriers within yourself you have
built against it.*

* RUMI

*If you have come here to help me, you are wasting your
time. But if you have come because your liberation is
bound up with mine, then let us work together*

* ABORIGINAL ACTIVIST GROUP,
Queensland, 1970s

The longtime prisoner and meditator Jarvis Jay Masters was
in the exercise yard at San Quentin when a seagull landed
in a puddle, and he saw a large young inmate pick up a stone to
throw at it. The unspoken rule in the yard was to mind your own
business—the smallest incident could turn violent—but Jarvis
immediately raised his arm to stop him. Outraged, the young
man shouted, "What you doing?" Everybody watching expected a fight. But Jarvis spontaneously responded, "That bird
has my wings." The younger man muttered and shook his head,
but somehow the tension dissipated. And for days afterward,

inmates came up to Jarvis to ask, "What did you mean by that, Jarvis?"

Something in us knows what Jarvis Masters meant. Whenever we pay close attention to another life, whether it's a person, our dog, a favorite plant, or a bird, this being begins to feel like part of us; it matters to us. We share the same wings, the same longing to live fully and freely. Yet we're also familiar with trance, when preoccupation, judgment, or feeling threatened makes it easy to distance ourselves, especially from those we don't know and who are different from us.

Trance makes them "Unreal Others" rather than subjective, feeling beings like ourselves. In trance, we can read the daily news of suffering—homes lost in floods, refugee families being turned away, another death in the opioid epidemic, the suicide of a gay teen—without registering the reality of these lives. "Isn't it awful," we might say, or "There but for the grace of God go I," and then turn back to our pressing business.

But of course, strangers aren't the only Unreal Others. The more stressed and reactive we are, the more even those we consider most dear can become unreal. Just as we can block our sense of their basic goodness, our hearts can close to defend us from their vulnerability. When we numb ourselves to their hurts and fears, we lose our ability to respond with warmth and tenderness.

And yet each of us has the potential to bring the spirit of "that bird has my wings" to all beings: This realization brings the happiness of being truly openhearted, and it is the hope for healing our planet. In this chapter, we'll explore how the radical compassion awakened in RAIN dissolve the trance of Unreal Othering.

EVOLUTIONARY ROOTS OF UNREAL OTHERS

Our deep conditioning to perceive Unreal Others emerged in service of survival. For millions of years, our earliest ancestors lived in small, isolated groups, where familiarity meant safety and any stranger was a potential threat. These groups called themselves "the people," or "humans." Other groups were "less than human," enemies to be hated and/or feared. And because "the people" were different and superior, they did not hesitate to attack and violate other groups: If they're not human, we can hurt them, steal from them, enslave them, kill them.

Then about seventy thousand years ago, humans entered a cognitive revolution marked by a dramatic leap in language, communication, and collaboration. Internally, this correlated with a radical spurt in brain development, culminating in the capacities of the prefrontal cortex for mindfulness and reason, empathy and compassion, and calming or regulating the reactions of our survival brain.

As the cognitive revolution spurred the growth of communication among human societies, it created a crucial evolutionary trajectory: our unfolding toward an interdependent global community. And yet in the most primitive parts of our brain, the Unreal Other persists, now working against our survival and ensnaring us in a regressive and toxic trance: It fuels institutionalized racism, classism, the oppression of refugees and other marginalized humans, unimaginable cruelty to nonhuman animals, war, and a mindless destruction of our earth's ecosystem.

Yet even as our ancient survival brain perpetuates the trance of Unreal Other, our evolved prefrontal cortex gives us the tools to undo it. Both as individuals and as a society, we have the capacity to recognize the biases that have kept us below the line. Once they are conscious, we become more able to respond from an awake and inclusive heart.

REFLECTION: BRINGING IMPLICIT BIAS ABOVE THE LINE

"Implicit bias" is the scientific term for the unconscious or semiconscious ways we stereotype individuals or groups, depending on our social conditioning. Please consider the following reflection as an opportunity for self-understanding, not as fuel for guilt and self-judgment.

Bring to mind the following groups of people:

- Those of a different race from you
- Different ethnic group or nationality
- Different religion
- Different sexual orientation
- Different gender identity
- Different ability (disability)
- Different social class
- Different political view

If possible, consider a few individuals you know from each. As you do, honestly notice any subtle judgments that emerge. Are they less—or more!—intelligent, ethical, attractive, loving, spiritual, or capable than yourself? Imagine that your child or someone else close to you has started dating someone from these groups. Notice your reactions in your body, because they may be more discernible than a mental expression of bias. As you review, also note the following: Are you inclined to blame the group for in some way being bad or wrong or causing harm?

Psychologists and neuroscientists who have tested implicit bias have shown that it can even be directed at the ability or worth of our own group.

Archbishop Desmond Tutu, winner of the Nobel Peace Prize for his work to end apartheid, tells a memorable story about his own discovery:

I went to Nigeria when I was working for the World Council of Churches, and I was due to fly to Jos. And so I go to Lagos airport and I get onto the plane and the two pilots in the cockpit are both black. And whee, I just grew inches. You know, it was fantastic because we had been told that blacks can't do this. And we have a smooth takeoff and then we hit the mother and father of turbulence. I mean, it was quite awful, scary. Do you know, I can't believe it, but the first thought that came to my mind was "Hey, there's no white men in that cockpit. Are those blacks going to be able to make it?" And of course, they obviously made it—here I am. But the thing is, I had not known that I was damaged to the extent of thinking that somehow actually what those white people who had kept drumming into us in South Africa about our being inferior, about our being incapable, it had lodged somewhere in me.

Early mindfulness researchers proposed that a key impact of mindfulness practice is the reduction of automatic processing. This is supported by more recent findings that mindfulness practice reduces implicit age and race bias. Say you have the associations that black is bad and old is bad. Mindfulness loosens these associations, enabling you to notice and question them, so that you see a person of color or an elderly person more clearly, with fewer distortions from societally conditioned bias. This frees you to recognize your shared vulnerability, your shared belonging.

Challenging our conditioning extends to the whole array of preconceived notions we might have about other peoples. It also extends to our tendency to feel separate from and more intrinsically valuable than nonhuman animals.

I experienced an awakening from this assumed superiority many years ago when I was leading a spring retreat in the Blue Ridge Mountains. The meditation center was located near a large farm, and during our early morning sitting we could hear sounds of cows lowing in distress, grieving for the calves that had recently been taken from them. (In the meat and dairy industry, farmers separate calves from their mothers as soon as possible in order to impregnate the mothers again.) With all mammals, there's a deep mother-child attachment, and now, for the first time, I could imagine the excruciating pain of those mothers and babes. Others did too. So we started to include the cows and calves in our daily heart meditation. Connecting to the reality of the enormous suffering caused by industrial farming, both then and increasingly over the following years, led me to a plant-based (vegan) diet.

The steps of RAIN allow us to recognize and undo the Unreal Othering that closes our hearts to other living beings. The mindfulness of RAIN asks, "What's it like being you?" and cultivates genuine understanding. The compassion of RAIN allows us to respond to others from a heart that says, "That bird has my wings."

TAKING IN ANOTHER BEING: RECOGNIZING AND ALLOWING

We practice the first step of RAIN when we look at other beings with the intention to Recognize whatever is happening with them at the moment—their mood or emotions, energy level, way of expressing themselves, appearance. Then, with whatever initially calls our attention, we pause and Allow. We include without judging.

A video I saw recently offers a beautiful illustration of the impact of Recognizing and Allowing.

Called *Look Beyond Borders*, it was made in 2016 as part of a study that paired a few of the millions of refugees who were arriving in Europe with people from their host countries. The video shows them being seated facing each other and asked to gaze quietly into each other's eyes for four minutes. First we see some nervous smiles, some laughter, tears. And then, after the silence, the camera focuses on a woman from Berlin as she speaks to the Syrian man facing her. "Are you alone here, or with your family?" "Alone," he answers softly. He pauses and adds, "It's life. Sometimes nice, sometimes, not good." Then their time is up; they rise to their feet and hug each other tightly. They had become real to each other.

This is the power of the non-judging mindful presence of Recognize and Allow. But what if you're practicing and judgment does come up? Instead of starting to judge yourself, simply bring RAIN inward, Recognizing and Allowing the judging thought, Investigating and feeling its energy in the body, and then offering care to whatever you find.

Seeing that "it's just a thought" clears the way for the next steps of RAIN, allowing you to go on to Investigation—which, as we will see, can dramatically loosen judgment.

REFLECTION: GAZING INTO ANOTHER'S EYES

This is one of the most valuable trainings I've found for dissolving trance. You might try it if you have a partner, family member, or friend who is willing to explore it with you.

—◌—

Sit face-to-face with knees almost touching and close your eyes. Take a few long, deep breaths, relax any obvious tension, and allow yourselves to settle and become present. Reflect on your mutual intention to offer a sustained, open, and nonjudgmental attention to each other. After about a minute, open your eyes. Sit for five minutes gazing into each other's eyes. Simply Recognize (notice) whatever experience arises and Allow it, let be. Afterward, take some time for each of you to share what you experienced.

DEEPENING OUR ATTENTION
TO THE OTHER: INVESTIGATING
AND NURTURING

Ruby Sales is a veteran of the civil rights movement and a life-long social activist with a focus on spiritually based community building. In a beautiful interview with Krista Tippett, I heard her describe a turning point on her path.

One morning Ruby was having her hair done, and the daughter of her hairdresser came in from what was clearly a long night hustling on the streets—exhausted, with sores on her body, on drugs. And Ruby, seeing her, suddenly felt called to ask a simple question, "Where does it hurt?" At these words, years of pent-up pain began to pour out. This young woman had been traumatized by sexual abuse since childhood. She had kept it all inside, not even letting her own mother know. Listening to her, Ruby realized she needed a larger way to do her work, a way of paying attention to the inner life of how we live in the world that gets to the root of pain and awakens our true understanding.

"Where does it hurt?" Now, as Ruby talks about racism, she not only talks about the pain of people of color. She also focuses on what she calls the spiritual crisis of white America. She speaks about "the forty-five-year-old person in Appalachia who is dying at a young age, who feels like they've been eradicated because whiteness is so much smaller today than it was yesterday," and "the white person in Massachusetts who's heroin-addicted because they feel that their lives have no meaning." Ruby is calling for a theology of love that purposefully seeks to understand—and care about—even those who might be seen as enemies.

Investigation reveals the vulnerability that naturally arouses Nurturing. Asking "Where does it hurt?" or more broadly, "What's it like being you?" quiets our reactive survival brain and awakens empathy, understanding, and care.

For Valarie Kaur, a civil rights lawyer, social activist, and Sikh, this inquiry became particularly compelling in the days, months, and years following 9/11. After the Twin Towers fell, the first person to be killed in a hate crime was a Sikh who was like an uncle to her. The killer was a man who called himself a patriot and said he'd decided to "go out and shoot some towel heads" in revenge.

Valarie was devastated and terrified. She had a young son who wears the traditional Sikh turban, and she feared for his life. "He's seen as a terrorist," she said, "just as black people are seen as criminals and women as property." In the midst of her fear, she reflected deeply on the best response to this murder. Gradually, she realized that she didn't want her pain to harden into anger against an Unreal Other, and two questions emerged to guide her work:

Who have we not yet tried to love?
Can we wonder about and tend to their wounds?

She had turned her attention toward Investigate and Nurture.

Fifteen years after her adopted uncle was murdered, Valarie contacted his killer, Frank, in prison. Early in the call, Frank insinuated a connection between her uncle and the deaths on 9/11. Valarie had to steady herself, had to remember her deep intention to try to understand him. Then, at one point, she wondered out loud why he had agreed to speak with her. This was when Frank told her: "I am sorry for what I did. . . . One day when I go to heaven to be judged by God I will ask to see him [Valarie's uncle], and I will hug him and ask him for forgiveness."

Today Valarie speaks nationwide, promoting love as a foundation for our collective work toward social and economic justice. She models activism on the labor of birth, where the first essential step is to breathe into the pain. Here she is guiding us to a mindful, non-judging presence; a presence that seeks to understand and to bring our hearts fully to what is: Investigate and Nurture—wonder about others and tend to their wounds. Only then can we effectively engage the energy for radical change—to push a new life into the world. And Valarie continues to describe her goal in a very personal way: "One day you will see my son as your own, and protect him when I'm not there."

RAIN IN ACTION: FACING THE RACIAL DIVIDE

Love is often hard work, and when we're in conflict, we can regress into our survival brain in a flash. I discovered this some years ago during a meeting of a multiracial group in our local community. One moment I was sharing openly about some serious health problems, explaining why I hoped we might meet less frequently. The next moment I was hurt, angry, and stunned by the comments of an African American friend. She had responded with quiet anger to my request: "I'm disappointed . . . and not trusting your commitment to our group." Our meeting ended with us both upset and distanced.

How could she be so insensitive? Didn't she know how important this was to me? Hadn't I been involved for years in several groups addressing white privilege and racial injustice?

When I had some quiet time later in the day, RAIN kicked in—first to look at my own reactivity. I quickly Recognized and Allowed the feelings of "hurt" and "angry." Investigating, I could feel a sense of betrayal; I'd been vulnerable and trusting, sharing about my health, and then got slammed. The belief was "She doesn't understand, she doesn't care." Then Nurture: I placed a hand on my heart, breathed in and out of the hurt place, and mentally whispered, "It's okay, sweetheart." This familiar process calmed me down and gave me some space. But it was much harder to bring RAIN to my friend. I could Recognize and Allow that she was upset, but Investigation wasn't bearing fruit.

A week later, feeling stuck, I asked another friend (also a woman of color) for help in understanding why my group member been so angry. I told her I had tried to understand but just couldn't get why she'd reacted the way she had. My friend said, "Tara, for you, it was about spreading out some meetings. As a white person, these meetings are optional for you. For an African American woman in her situation, they feel like life or death."

In an instant, my awareness shifted. I recalled the times my friend had shared her concern about her grandson, who was in jail. I remembered her powerful blog post where she discussed feeling like a mother to all the African American men in the streets who were targets of racial violence. Our meetings were part of a larger process of healing racism, something her life was dedicated to, and we in the group were the friends and allies she trusted, had invested in. And now a white person was threatening to withdraw some of her energy. Not only that, but I was a white person with power, someone whose leadership was needed in racism work.

At this my heart broke open. Her experience as an African American woman had become more real to me.

There's a tendency in some spiritual communities to brush over differences with the belief "we're all really one." Yes, but people who have been marginalized (like people of color) live in a world that is far more dangerous than many white people know. I needed to really get it in my cells how my friend considered the young black men who were losing their lives in the streets: "These are my sons." And how it felt not to be able to rely on white people to stay with the ongoing and often messy work of racial healing.

When we talked a few days later, I was able to listen with full presence to how she experienced our conflict. She too had reflected deeply, and could see through my eyes and express her care. We hurt each other in that clash, but by being willing to stay engaged and deepen our attention, we brought our friendship closer.

In the months that followed, paying attention to differences helped me come more above the line on something else: my whiteness. I could see in retrospect how my friend's confrontation had triggered strong feelings of guilt—the chronic underlying sense that as a white person, I wasn't doing enough to eliminate racism.

My awareness of whiteness has become a continuing process of awakening to the assumptions and privileges that come with my skin color: That I could go into any store and not be viewed as a potential criminal. That I could buy a home in any neighborhood. That I'd have a good chance at getting jobs I was qualified for. I've also taken for granted that I'd receive good, respectful medical attention. And perhaps more subtly, when it would help me to change the schedule of our group meetings, I could simply ask for what I wanted. This was an entitlement that I as a white person, and as a person with power, had never questioned.

During this period of my waking up around whiteness, my husband, Jonathan, and I took a vacation. One afternoon we decided to swim from the beach to a small island some distance away. Swimming out was a joy: My strokes were confident and steady; I felt tireless and graceful. But returning was different. I quickly became fatigued, and when we finally got back, I was thirsty, exhausted, and humbled. I hadn't realized that currents had carried me out to the island and then worked against my return. And so it is with the currents of a white-dominant culture: They make life unimaginably easier for white people and painfully difficult for people of color.

REFLECTION: "IS THIS PERSON REAL TO ME?"

We've been looking at how we create Unreal Others. It's important to realize that, especially when we're stressed, our habits of Unreal Othering apply even to those closest to us—our brother, child, mother, friend, and work colleague. We are trying to "get through the day," and they are making things worse or better or playing bit parts, irrelevant to our concerns. We're just not there; our hearts are closed. If we want to relate more reliably with presence and compassion, we need to bring the habitual trance of Unreal Other above the line. Our starting place is to pay closer attention to our everyday encounters.

—⊖—

Take a few long, deep breaths, relax any obvious tension in your body, and arrive in presence. Now review your day, or the last couple of days. Remind yourself of someone you spent time with. Be curious about how attuned you were. How "real" did this person seem to you? Did you notice

- what kind of mood they were in?
- how they were feeling physically?
- what was important to them at the time you connected?
- what they might have been worried or anxious about?
- if they were relaxed, comfortable, and open with you?
- if they were tense and defensive with you?
- whether anything in the interaction was difficult for them?

Investigate without judgment, and as you deepen your attention, notice if the person you're reflecting on becomes more multifaceted, interesting, and real. And notice your heart's response to this person. Before ending, you might think of someone you're going to be spending time with soon. Imagine entering this next encounter with the inquiry "What's it like being you?" Or, if they've been having difficulty, "Where does it hurt?"

CAN YOU HAVE TOO MUCH COMPASSION?

But perhaps right now you're feeling the barriers going up. "I'm already extremely sensitive," people tell me. "If I let in everybody else's pain, I'll be overwhelmed." I'm often asked about "compassion fatigue," exhaustion from encountering so much suffering in our world.

It's true that many people, especially social activists and those in the helping professions, become burned out. But it's likely that the real culprit is empathy, not compassion. Empathy is our capacity to feel the emotions of others and/or take the perspective of other people. But therein lies a trap: If we become too distressed by their suffering, we may not have the cognitive or emotional resources to help them.

Compassion begins with empathy, but *the crucial element of mindfulness protects us from merging or identifying with the pain.* Empathy alone can lead to burnout, but the mindfulness and care inherent in compassion foster resilience, connectedness, and action.

Neuroscientists have even been able to detect clear differences in how these two states are processed in the brain. Empathy activates areas linked to emotion, self-awareness, and pain. Compassion stimulates areas associated with care and nurturing, and also those connected to learning, decision making, and the brain's reward system. It also stimulates secretion of oxytocin, the "bonding hormone" released during lovemaking and while nursing a baby. We feel warmth and connection—positive feelings that mobilize our energy and make us more capable of helping effectively.

CULTIVATING COMPASSION WITH RAIN

For Mitch, a member of our meditation community, the most difficult part of his father's decline into Alzheimer's was his mother's suffering. "It's like ongoing and countless deaths," she told him. Mitch was the only one of his siblings who lived nearby, and he visited his parents regularly. As his father sank into confusion, Mitch began to dread the obligatory time in their small condo. Sometimes his mother's loneliness and despair would flood him, and he'd leave feeling overwhelmed, exhausted, and helpless. But just as often—especially when he was stressed or busy—he'd feel robotic, cold, and distant. Either way, he was filled with guilt about not really showing up.

At a daylong workshop, Mitch explored bringing RAIN to his painful mix of feelings. The day started with sharing in small groups, and Mitch talked about his own sorrow at losing the father he knew, about his mother's grief, and also about his guilt—"I'm being dragged into a bottomless pit, and I don't want to be there."

As group members began to practice RAIN on their own, Mitch focused on Recognizing and Allowing his own empathic distress: how he was feeling his mother's feelings, as well as his own reactivity of overwhelm and withdrawal. He took his time, mindfully naming the emotions—fear, grief, guilt, helplessness—and with each, Allowing it to be there.

Mindfulness also allowed him to deepen into Investigation, discovering how his sense of failure appeared in his body, feeling the squeezing in his chest and the twisting in his belly. Observing this intensity, he began Nurture by whispering, "It's okay, breathe, relax." He then remembered a recent visit that was particularly upsetting: His mom had yelled at his dad for walking outside in his pajamas and then crumpled in tears of remorse. He was ashamed of the helplessness he'd felt and how he'd hated being there.

Again he gently sent the message "It's okay, breathe, relax," and then repeated it several times. A deep clutching inside him loosened, and some space opened up. What followed was an image of himself hugging his mom as she was weeping. He was holding her in tenderness, and after some moments this loving space included his father, too. As he told me later, "After all these months of being so upset about their situation, I had some moments of simply caring about them. It was the first time . . . just caring."

Perhaps you've experienced this too—being so worried or overwhelmed or reactive to another's suffering that there was no room for the pure experience of care. At these times, RAIN can help us return to the tenderness of our heart.

RAIN TRANSFORMS EMPATHY INTO COMPASSION

Recognize: Brings mindfulness to painful empathic feelings and reactions like fear, grief, guilt, shame, aversion, anger, numbness, or tightness.

Allow: Loosens our identification with the feelings and gives us more space to witness rather than react.

Investigate: As we then inquire gently and more directly contact the empathic feelings in our body, our tenderness and caring naturally arise.

Nurture: The fullness of compassion manifests as we feel and express care for ourselves and for all who experience suffering.

After the RAIN: As we rest in this compassionate presence, we become familiar with the natural openness, radiance, and tenderness of our heart.

The openhearted caring of After the RAIN transformed Mitch's visit with his parents the next day. He was immediately struck by the trap his mom was in. He had a practice that he now knew could help him, but she was alone all day with her overwhelming feelings and needed more emotional support than he could possibly provide. She also needed more day-to-day help in caring for his dad. Over the next weeks, Mitch put his energies behind getting her into an Alzheimer's support group and bringing in some part-time nursing care. His mother, like all of us, needed to feel that she belonged to a community of care that could help her carry her grief and loss. And as

Mitch felt less stuck in overwhelm or guilt, his response to his parents became increasingly simple and clear: He could let himself be touched by their suffering and respond with care.

I find it helpful to use breathing as an image of compassion. We need to breathe in—mindfully taking in and connecting with what we and others are feeling. There is no presence and no potential for compassion if we don't fully contact the reality of these emotions. And we need to breathe out—actively expressing our care and connecting with the larger space that unfolds when we feel loving and/or loved. Only the vastness of our heartspace has room for the intensity of human emotions.

This truth is embodied in the Tibetan compassion practice called Tonglen, which literally means "taking in and sending out." With the in breath, we mindfully take in suffering; with the out breath, we send out our care. Like RAIN, Tonglen cultivates the two wings of awareness: mindful contact with the reality of suffering, and an active expression of nurturing.

THAT BIRD HAS MY WINGS . . . FOR REAL

Pity often masquerades as compassion—as if Jarvis Masters had thought, "Oh, you poor bird!" Pity positions us as separate and above the other person. We're sorry for them and want to help, but they are still "other." With true compassion, we feel the other person's experience as our shared human vulnerability. Our urge to help is not "doing good"; it's like tending to a wound on our own body. In the words of the aboriginal activist group in Queensland that open this chapter, "If you have come here to help me, you are wasting your time. But if you have come because your liberation is bound up with mine, then let us work together." True healing grows from the wisdom of interdependence.

While volunteering in a nursing home for the destitute in Peru, a young man named Phil found himself waiting for hours in an emergency room with an old man who had broken his hip. All Phil could do was keep him company, and he felt helpless at not being able to relieve his pain. At one point, someone handed the man a bread roll. He immediately broke off half and tried to give it to Phil. Surprised, Phil refused to take it, but the man pushed the bread into his hand, motioning him to eat. And so he did, bewildered and humbled, as the old man looked quite pleased to be sharing his meal.

This experience radically shifted Phil's understanding of compassion. The elderly man was no longer an Unreal Other, a passive, unfortunate person to be helped. And Phil was not the privileged helper, doing something nice. They were in it together, lives linked in mutual care and belonging.

So often we imagine the spiritual path as one of discipline and difficulty. Yes, compassion does take training; as in the meditation below, we are consciously developing compassion as an enduring trait. Yet because compassion is our evolutionary potential, the more we move in this direction, the more we feel a sense of homecoming. Radical compassion springs from the very roots of our being. When we are living from this source, we spontaneously respond to our world with the wisdom "That bird has my wings."

MEDITATION: THE RAIN OF COMPASSION—"WHAT'S IT LIKE BEING YOU?"

There are times when this compassion practice may be inappropriate. If you are struggling with trauma-related fear, unrelenting depression, or severe psychological imbalance, this practice may cause emotional flooding or a sense of being stuck. Should you choose to practice and at any point feel overwhelmed, discontinue, and seek guidance from a spiritual teacher, therapist, or trusted guide in finding what will best help you move toward healing.

—⊝—

Sit in a way that allows you to be relaxed and alert. Let go of any habitual tension, and allow your body and mind to settle.

Take a few moments to scan through family members and/or friends who are close to you, and choose someone who you know is having a difficult time. Connect with your intention to awaken compassion toward this person.

Recognize: Become aware of whatever is most prominent about this person as you reflect on their current challenges. You might recall a mood they're often in, something about their appearance, a regular activity of theirs, or the tone of recent communications.

Allow: Let your sense of this person—of how they are living, feeling, or expressing themselves—be just as it is, without adding any judgment.

Investigate: With gentleness, curiosity, and interest, now ask more deeply about their experience. Imagine feeling with their heart, viewing the world from their perspective. You might use some of the following questions to explore "What's it like being you?"

What life circumstances are most distressing to you?
What fears, disappointments, or hurts are you carrying?
What are you believing about yourself?
How does this life situation—and the emotions of fear, hurt, anger, or shame—feel in your heart and body?
Where inside do you feel most vulnerable?
What does that vulnerable place most want or need right now—from others? From yourself?

Nurture: Keeping this person and their vulnerability in your heart, expand your awareness to your whole body and to the sounds and space around you. From that inclusive heartspace, feel this being as part of you and offer what is needed. Is it acceptance? Being held? Forgiveness? Company? Understanding? You might also offer care energetically, as a flow of warmth, as an image, or through words. Imagine this person receiving and letting in your care, and envision them healed, happy, and well.

(If you'd like to try using the breath in this meditation, breathe in as you Investigate, taking in the reality of this person's experience. As you Nurture, breathe out your offering of space, care, or whatever else is needed.)

Widening the Circles: Now enlarge the field of compassion to include all those who experience the same suffering. If the person you are reflecting on is grieving a loss, connect with and offer care to all those grieving loss. If this person feels like a failure, connect with and offer care to all those who suffer this way. Sense the willingness of your heart to be touched by pain (breathing in), and the vastness of loving awareness that is here, as you offer care to all beings (breathing out).

After the RAIN: Let go of all ideas of others, and notice the qualities of heart and presence within you. Is there a sense of openness? Tenderness? Love? Whatever you find, let go and rest there.

PRACTICE: ON-THE-STREETS COMPASSION

Whenever you become aware of suffering, you can practice compassion. You might be online and see a story about a refugee family. You might be driving on a highway and see a car accident. You might be at an AA meeting, listening as someone describes their struggle with alcoholism.

—⊖—

Right on the spot, you can follow these simple steps (adapted from the Tonglen practice):

- Pause, and connect with your intention toward compassion.
- For several slow and full breaths, silently breathe in their pain, allowing yourself to imagine and feel what they are experiencing.
- With the out breath, breathe out your care—wishing for their relief and that they be held in the openness of loving awareness.

- If you feel yourself resisting, turned off, or afraid of the pain, breathe for yourself, and then, if it's possible, return to the person who is suffering.

QUESTIONS AND RESPONSES

I wish I had more compassion, but the truth is I'm pretty caught up in my own problems. I just don't seem to have much authentic caring for others.

Thank you for your honesty, and please know that many others feel the same way. One of the reasons I so often share the image of compassion as widening circles is that it reminds us that compassion for our own life is at the center. If we are having a hard time and don't hold our own vulnerability with care, it's harder to embrace others with a full and wise presence.

You write that you wish you had more compassion. I remember the Dalai Lama once said that while he wasn't always good at practicing compassion, he cared about it. In other words, even when our heart isn't open, what matters is that deep down *we care about caring*. You can trust that caring is intrinsic to who you are.

Let your intention be to offer the caring presence of RAIN to the pain of your own difficulties. Investigate and sense the most painful feelings you are experiencing—maybe fear or hurt or self-judgment— and make sure to feel them fully in your body, as that will awaken authentic self-compassion. Offer Nurturing to yourself, and then explore widening the circles: staying connected to the sense of inner vulnerability, bring to mind others who might be experiencing similar life problems and similar feelings. Extend the presence of RAIN to them: Imagine and let yourself be touched by their pain, and then offer them Nurturing too. Sense how we are in it together; we really do have each other's wings! You'll find that in time this practice of widening the circles awakens a very sincere and tender caring for all of us.

I've tried the on-the-streets compassion practice, but I find that I just get angry or scared and then shut down. What should I do?

Again, getting reactive in offering compassion outward is a signal that you first need to bring the RAIN of compassion inward to your own experience. Sometimes it won't take long to Recognize and Allow your own reactions, say becoming angry at how you or another is being treated; getting judgmental about how you are treating yourself; feeling fear when someone acts aggressively. Investigating helps contact in your body the vulnerability underneath your reaction, and then Nurturing can soothe and comfort. This may give you the presence and bandwidth to sense the realness of another's distress and offer your prayer and care.

But if you need more time for self-compassion, be patient. You can trust that the more often you offer a gesture of kindness to your own heart, the more readily you'll find yourself responding to those around you with a natural openheartedness and care.

I want to stop othering, but how am I supposed to feel compassion for people who hate me for being white? For instance . . . Muslims or black people who consider me the enemy? It feels like a bad othering dance none of us can step out of!

We are all subject to our societal conditioning, and if we don't address this on the group level, we miss the real healing that is possible.

If you are feeling hated or blamed, the first step is to bring acceptance and compassion to whatever is arising inside you—perhaps your own sense of hurt or anger at being the target of others. While you can begin to do this on your own, it's invaluable to find an affinity group of white people dedicated to waking up—to seeing unconscious bias and bringing an honest, caring attention to their shared conditioning. By collectively holding your Unreal Othering with compassion, you will gain insights and inspiration not available when you are practicing on your own.

Once you've enlarged your self-awareness, it's time to make the effort to connect with people from different races to understand their realities and the suffering they are living with.

I saw a video of African American CNN commentator Van Jones being confronted by a young white man who was enraged by the focus on racial violence against black people when there had just been a killing of a white police officer by an African American. Van responded, "If you cry just as much when that black man died in that police car, and I cry just as much when that horrible bigot shot down the police . . . If you're crying and I'm crying just as much, and we're crying together . . . then we can find a way to get our cops to be better and our kids better. . . ." What had started as a hostile encounter ended with mutual respect and a warm hug.

In compassion training that addresses groups of Unreal Others, it's natural and skillful to first deepen our understanding and healing by joining with those who feel safe and are easiest to relate to—affinity groups for just people of color, whites, Muslims, those of particular sexual orientations or gender identities, etc. But to continue evolving, we then need to wonder, "Where does it hurt?" and extend our care to widening circles. People of different and conflicting races, religions and political views, need to spend time with each other and awaken their care for each other's suffering. We need to cry together, as Van says, to create a better world.

I'm white and deeply distressed about racism. Yet the more I see my white privilege, the more self-conscious I get around my black friends and the guiltier I feel. Clearly this doesn't help, but I don't know what to do.

Seeing white privilege—all the often hidden ways white people in contemporary societies benefit from their skin color—is essential if we are to evolve into a more just and compassionate world. But what makes white privilege so insidious is that it's a pervasive societal conditioning, rather than a personal flaw. You can't choose what color you are or what society you are in or what biases you are fed. This is not a matter of blaming individuals. It's not your fault, and as you indicate, guilt and self-consciousness do not contribute to healing. And yet, when white people start facing the ongoing suffering experienced by people of color, and the unconscious part they themselves play in perpetuating this suffering, they can become paralyzed by white guilt.

For the first eight months in one of my diversity groups, I felt anxious, awkward, and inauthentic every time I spoke. After one meeting that I hosted, I said my good-byes, returned to my empty living room, and realized I felt like an outsider in this circle, as if I didn't belong. RAIN helped me contact a raw place of shame, a part of me that felt as if just being white were hurtful and that I could never do enough to right the horrors inflicted on generations of people of color. Of course I felt anxious and separate. I felt basically bad! I had encountered my own white guilt before, in a white affinity group, and now that it was again in full awareness, I was able to Nurture the place in me that took racism personally. While it took time, realizing that it was part of my conditioned identity as a white person—that it wasn't my personal fault— actually freed me to be more engaged and real in the group. It's helped me to be a better ally in antiracism efforts and to develop some friendships that I continue to cherish.

While we can't choose our skin color or our society, we can choose how we want to respond to the suffering of racism. To varying degrees, every one of us suffers from racism, and we suffer whether we're identified with dominant or nondominant populations. There's no freedom—spiritual or other—if we don't pay attention. Here I think of Valarie Kaur's wonderful call to action: We need to breathe with the pain of racism—feel it, bring compassion to it—and push, actively engage, for change. Breathe and push!

ELEVEN

Four Remembrances: Living with an Awake Heart

Wisdom tells me I am nothing. Love tells me I am everything. And between the two, my life flows.

• SRI NISARGADATTA

More than twenty-five years ago, I went to a weekend retreat led by the Zen master Thich Nhat Hanh with my dear friend and fellow teacher Luisa Montero-Diaz. We were delighted that Thay (as he is known) was teaching nearby, and also delighted to be taking time off from our busy lives of teaching and parenting to have two days together. But my brightest memory is of how the retreat ended.

Thay asked all of us to find partners, and Luisa and I quickly paired up. He began by instructing us to bow to our partner, acknowledging that each of us saw the Buddha in the other. Next we were to hug each other and then, while we embraced, take three long, deep breaths. During the first breath, we were to reflect: "I am going to die." During the second:

"You are going to die." And during the third: "And we have just these precious moments together."

When Luisa and I released our embrace, we stood together in silence. I was filled with tenderness for her; she was infinitely dear, unique, and wonderful. And I could feel the same warmth for me emanating from her smile and shining eyes. We stayed in this openhearted presence as we began to speak, as we said our good-byes to other retreatants, as we walked through the pine trees to our car, and as we laughed and shared stories and silence during the drive home.

Everything we most value—love, creativity, play, beauty, wisdom—can only be experienced here and now. Yet it's so easy to race through life, forgetting that "we have just these precious moments." The gift of RAIN is that it reminds us to pause, reconnects us with a wise and compassionate presence, and allows us to align our lives with our hearts.

As we complete our journey together, I want to share the four remembrances that guide me in daily life. You'll find that each can bring alive your natural care and intelligence at times when you are likely to be caught in reactivity. These informal practices are drawn from RAIN and can be woven into stressful moments at work, difficult conversations, and any other situation where you want support in living true to yourself. They are the nourishment for our continued unfolding.

If you practice the four remembrances regularly, you'll find that the qualities of heart/mind you most value, like openheartedness and equanimity, become available, strong, and steady.

As you transform these uplifting states of mind into enduring traits, the potential of your future self will blossom in daily life.

THE FOUR REMEMBRANCES

Pause for Presence

Say Yes to What's Here

Turn Toward Love

Rest in Awareness

PAUSE FOR PRESENCE

Father Gregory Boyle, a Jesuit priest and author known for his work with gangs in Los Angeles, tells this story: It's after Sunday morning service, and he's in his office with a short window to get through his mail before performing a baptism. In walks Carmen, a gang member and occasional prostitute. Plopping down on a couch, she starts rambling: She needs help, she went to Catholic school, she's been to countless rehab centers, she's known nationwide. He's got his eye on the clock; she's all over the place, and it's now five minutes before the family arrives for the baptism.

All of a sudden Carmen looks directly at him, and her eyes pool with tears. She says she started heroin after dropping out of high school and has been trying to stop ever since. Then she says slowly and clearly, "I . . . am . . . a . . . disgrace." Father Greg writes, "Suddenly, her shame meets mine. For when

Carmen walked through that door, I had mistaken her for an interruption."

Most of us know what it's like to be on our way somewhere else—to assume that whatever's happening here is just an obstacle to move through. Others become an interruption, but that's not all. When we skim the surface of our days, we lose touch with our own heart and awareness.

I have a favorite saying posted in my office: "To be kind, you must swerve regularly from your path." The challenge of this teaching was highlighted in a famous piece of social science research popularly known as the Good Samaritan study. The question was this: What affects the likelihood that we'll help a stranger in need? In one part of the study, the researchers asked seminary students (surely people dedicated to service!) to prepare a short sermon on the biblical story of the Good Samaritan. The seminarians were then to go to another building to present their talk. Some of them were told they had plenty of time, others that they were already late. Their route took them right past a doorway where a man (an actor) sat slumped over, coughing, and obviously in difficulty. The key finding was this: The students who thought they were late were much less likely to stop and ask if they could help—even as they rushed to speak about the Good Samaritan.

Especially when strong emotions like fear, shame, and anger are running the show, we'll do almost anything rather than be right here feeling our raw and unpleasant feelings. When we're caught in our reactive trance, it's as though we were on a bicycle pedaling away from the present moment, and the more stressed we feel, the faster we pedal.

Whatever your deepest regrets about your life—ignoring

your children, addictive bingeing, causing an accident, staying in an abusive relationship—all arise from being trapped inside a reactive trance. When we're in trance, we're unable to swerve, unable to respond to ourselves or to others with kindness.

Pausing for presence begins in RAIN when we Recognize and Allow what is here, and stop pedaling. We are learning to let go of the habitual controls—of all our strategies for avoiding unpleasantness and discomfort, and grasping after pleasure. Practicing these pauses informally throughout the day might be uncomfortable or scary, refreshing or relieving. No matter what it feels like, pausing is the gateway to presence— to living aligned with our hearts.

REMEMBRANCE: PAUSE FOR PRESENCE

For now, set your intention to pause in just one or two situations of moderate stress and reactivity. It might be when you see a flurry of new emails needing a response; when you're worrying about an upcoming deadline; about to enter a demanding meeting; or feeling irritated with a friend, colleague, or family member.

The pause itself is simple. Stop whatever you're doing, become still, and take a moment to Recognize and Allow whatever emotions and thoughts are present. Then take three to five long, deep breaths. With each, match the length of the inhale and exhale: Breathe in fully, filling your chest and lungs, and then release with a long, slow out breath. When you've finished, notice if anything has changed, and then continue with your day.

Gradually expand the number of situations in which you practice an intentional pause, including those that involve more emotional triggering. In time, you'll be able to pause in a wide range of situations, and you'll have more access to your inner clarity, resilience, and heart.

SAY YES TO WHAT'S HERE

The holy man in chapter 6 posed a crucial question to those seeking spiritual healing: "What are you unwilling to feel?" Often what keeps us pedaling away from presence is our fear of painful or unfamiliar experiences. Yet by saying yes, we can bring the places that most need our compassionate attention into the light of awareness. Saying yes opens the door to genuine trust, confidence, and healing.

I saw this most poignantly in the life and death of a close friend and beloved Buddhist teacher, Cheri Maples, who inspired me and many others with her "yes."

For the first weeks after Cheri crashed her bike into a moving van, doctors had doubted she could survive the extensive and multiple traumas to her body. Should she make it, they were certain that Cheri, a lifelong athlete who found her deepest joy in outdoor adventure, would never walk again. Before taking Buddhist vows, Cheri had been a police officer, a social activist, and an assistant attorney general for the State of

Wisconsin. This fiercely independent woman would henceforth depend on the aid of others for moving from lying to sitting, for urinating, for bathing, for almost everything.

Yet when I visited her in the intensive rehabilitation unit where she spent many months, she was in good spirits—her naturally warm, interested, bright self. How was it possible that her life could take such a sudden sharp turn and that she could still be happy? As Cheri put it to me, "I have already faced the worst death; I can live with this."

Two years earlier, Cheri and her partner of nine years had gone through a wrenching breakup. Cheri spiraled into a depression that was entirely out of her control. She pulled away from her teaching and social activism, outdoor recreation and formal meditation practice. She isolated herself from all but a few friends. When we talked, she told me that something in her core had withered: "I've lost hope that I can feel close with the world."

Then, very slowly, her informal practice—the mindfulness and self-kindness of RAIN—took hold. She began acknowledging and saying yes to the worst death: the pain of losing love. To be clear, this was not a full-blown "yes," not an openhearted acceptance with no resistance. Rather, when she could, she'd contact the waves of loneliness, terror, and desolation and let them be there. Recognizing and Allowing. Saying yes. In time, the "yes" became increasingly filled with compassion.

Over many months, as Cheri opened her body and heart to the reality of loss and grieved deeply, the tentacles of depression gradually loosened. She emerged with a fresh sense of openness to life and a deep trust in her own resilience. Along with another good friend, we taught a retreat together, and

Cheri was filled with creativity and joie de vivre. She was, as she'd always been, courageously transparent about her vulnerabilities. She was saying yes to her life and living with an increasingly fearless heart.

Witnessing Cheri's healing reminded me of a teaching that captures the essence of Recognize and Allow: "Meet your edge and soften." Sometimes meeting our edge means recognizing a feeling of resentment or irritation or discouragement. At other times it's acknowledging the anguish and defeat that comes with a failing relationship, a life-threatening illness, or the suffering of a loved one. We soften by saying yes, letting go of resistance and allowing our experience to be just as it is. Because life serves up an ongoing stream of challenges great and small, this is an ongoing practice. Yet each time we meet our edge and soften, we become increasingly confident that we can handle whatever comes our way.

Just a week after our retreat, and six months after returning to her former active life, Cheri had the bike accident. Now she was facing another kind of death—loss of control over the most basic tasks of daily life. And yet this round was different. She knew how to meet her edge and soften: She could say yes to impermanence and loss; she could live with this death.

Saying yes expresses our heart's wisdom. Only when we open to reality as it is—without any resisting or grasping—can our heart and intelligence come fully alive. Only by saying yes to this moment can we respond to our own life and the lives of others with the courage of radical compassion.

REMEMBRANCE: SAY YES TO WHAT'S HERE

While we need to open to our deep fears and losses, we can develop our resilience and confidence if we first practice saying yes to moderate discomfort and unpleasantness. You might try saying yes when you have indigestion or a headache; when you are anxious about being late, annoyed that the car was left close to "empty," or disappointed at missing a dear one's wedding. Keep in mind that your "yes" is directed toward your own inner experience, not toward what someone else is doing. You are meeting your edge—any sense of emotional reactivity or inner conflict—and softening.

Here are some ways to begin:

- Whisper "yes" inwardly or say it softly out loud. Or alternate "yes" with "it's okay," "I consent," "this belongs," or any other word or phrase that conveys acceptance.
- Imagine sending the message of "yes" directly to the inner place of vulnerability, upset, discomfort, or pain.
- Make a gesture of bowing respectfully to the inner experience, or visualize yourself bowing.
- Meet the inner experience with a slight smile; let this form at your lips, and then try to feel the smile in your eyes and in your heart.

End by taking some moments to notice if there is any shift in your body, heart, or mind.

TURN TOWARD LOVE

Like many of us, Cheri had never been very good at asking for or receiving help. She was impatient and used to getting things done ... quickly. Now, after her accident, she found that saying yes meant surrendering to her utter dependency. She had to accept being seen by others in states of mental confusion, acute pain, emotional distress, and powerlessness. She had to accept having people she didn't know handling her traumatized body. She had to accept that to be moved to an upright position took a long time, accept that she had to ask for absolutely anything she wanted or needed.

Saying yes to the rawness and depths of vulnerability opened her to something she had never imagined. On the day I visited her, Cheri told me about a nurse's aide who came one evening to bathe her: "I had never seen her before. She was quiet, a small woman from Guatemala—not someone who filled the air with talk. But every part of bathing me, from massaging my head to soaping my neck and back, was a gesture of love. She wasn't just helping me; she was loving me. She was an angel, bathing me in love!"

This aide appeared only once, but in fact Cheri was bathed in love that was flowing in from all directions—from each prayerful card and thoughtful gift, from the devoted advocacy and unceasing nurturing of her close-in support team, from the circle of healers who visited weekly.

As I saw that day sitting by her bedside, Cheri's "yes" had created the space not only for receiving love but also for offering it freely and with good cheer. When an aide came by to take her vitals, he and Cheri celebrated a win by the Packers (Cheri's home team). When an older nurse appeared, Cheri softly asked how her husband was doing, and I saw how the woman moved in closer to share details of his recent job loss. Cheri told me about brainstorming promotion ideas for a friend's new book and about her fears for a student whose son struggled with addiction.

This same openhearted spirit filled our time together. Cheri brought out her precious stash of ginger candies to share with me. We looked at photos from another recent visitor—her beloved dog Bear, who was lying by her side on her hospital bed. Then I took Bear's spot as a friend snapped pictures for our mutual buddies in D.C. We joked about my training to become her service dog.

All that day we were both aware that we had "just these precious moments." When I rose to depart that evening, we knew this might be the last time we were together in person, and it was. Yet our shared heartspace was large enough to hold our sorrow. We were able to love each other without holding back.

As you might have discovered, it can be easier to offer love openly when someone is gravely ill or in the face of a natural disaster or tragedy. Yet if we want to cultivate the *trait* of loving presence—if we want to embody and express it consistently in our lives—we need to practice turning toward love many times a day. We need to pay attention in ways that warm, soften, and open our hearts. This doesn't mean looking for a big emotional experience. Just the "turning toward" plants the seeds.

When I'm having a hard time, simply remembering the *idea* of kindness, or mentally saying the word "kindness," begins to soften me. Sometimes I might whisper a caring message to my-self and place my hands gently on my heart. Often I'll imagine feeling the Beloved kissing my brow, and as I feel filled with that loving presence, I'll offer care outward to others. All this might take just a few moments, and such moments may happen many times through the day.

I've found that what matters for myself and others is a sincere intention. Then, even if the body and mind are trapped in aversion, there's an opening for the tenderness and light of our heart to shine through.

REMEMBRANCE: TURN TOWARD LOVE

Set your intention to turn toward love when you become aware of feeling lonely, depressed, anxious, caught in self-judgment, or blaming others. Give yourself permission to experiment with different ways of reconnecting with love. Here are some possible approaches:

- Send a caring message or prayer to yourself (silently or whisper out loud). Examples: "May I be happy"; "May I feel safe"; "Please be kind"; "It's okay, sweetheart"; "I'm sorry and I love you"; "May I love myself into healing."
- Imagine receiving a caring message from a loved one or compassionate spiritual figure.
- Place one or both hands on your heart; hug yourself; place a comforting hand on your cheek; put your palms together in prayer.

- Imagine yourself surrounded by and held in warm light; imagine yourself being embraced by a loved one or by a compassionate spiritual figure; imagine you yourself are embracing your inner child.
- Imagine and feel what it's like to let in love. Visualize the eyes of a loved one who is feeling and expressing his or her care, and then sense your body allowing the warmth of that care to wash through you, to bathe you.
- Send your care to dear ones, others in your life, and those you don't know. You might do this through a message and/or image.

The more often you intentionally turn toward love—expressing it and letting it in—the more your natural care and compassion will arise spontaneously throughout the day.

REST IN AWARENESS

In the practice of RAIN, crucial moments of integration, healing, and freedom often emerge immediately *after* you've moved through the four intentional steps. That is why I've stressed the period called After the RAIN, when we simply notice and rest in presence. It is during this time of non-doing that we directly experience the openness, wakefulness, and tenderness of our true nature. These moments can reveal the formless radiance of consciousness itself, the essence of who we are.

Many people, however, skip or shortchange the invitation to "stop doing and rest in awareness." We are conditioned to move restlessly on to something else. The clock is still ticking; there's always more to do. As a result, both in meditation and in daily life, moments of pure being are rare. Yet if we were at the end of our life looking back, the experiences that would most matter—such as feeling at home with ourselves, connected to others, and fully alive—arise from this open presence.

If you're caught in an emotional tangle, it's difficult to become aware of the background of awareness itself. At such times, your attention naturally fixates on the foreground of obsessive thoughts, fears, and wants, and you'll benefit from reawakening mindfulness and compassion with the steps of RAIN. But when you've completed RAIN, or when in daily life you're relatively relaxed, the lens of perception is more open. Then it's easier to sense that behind the changing stream of images, sounds, and sensations, there's a background of consciousness.

Here's one of my favorite brief exercises: Stop reading, close your eyes, and for the next twenty seconds Try Not to Be Aware. Starting now!

Were you successful? It's likely you realized that you can't shut awareness off. Awareness is always here, always noticing what's happening. But because we're focused on the movie in our mind, emotions, or external objects, we are not aware of awareness itself.

Turning your attention from the sounds or sensations to that which is aware of them, and resting in that formless presence, allow for a radical shift in your own experience of being.

Recall the image of the Golden Buddha. Most of the time,

our sense of identity is hitched to our external coverings—our self-story, personality, defenses, wants, fears, achievements, and failures. These coverings are a natural part of who we are, but they don't reflect the wholeness of our being. Resting in awareness reconnects us to the vastness, beauty, and mystery of our existence. The formless awake space of awareness is the source of our love, wisdom, and creativity. It is the gold, the sacred essence of our life.

REMEMBRANCE: REST IN AWARENESS

Set your intention to rest in awareness at times when you are calm and quietly present. It might be when you lie down to sleep and can feel yourself unwinding; when you are listening to the sound of wind or rain; when you are looking at cloud formations or the intricacy of a flower; when you are with someone in comfortable silence. It might also be when you've arrived at your destination, right before getting out of the car. Or when you are standing and looking out a window.

Close your eyes, be still, and notice the foreground of what you are experiencing—the thoughts, sensations, images, sounds. Let everything be just as it is. Then notice your own presence, the formless awareness in the background. What is awareness? Can you sense the silence? The stillness? The openness that everything is happening in? Relax and rest in this awareness; *become* the awareness.

Often after just a few seconds, the mind re-fixates on

something in the foreground—or perhaps on a thought about what's next. This is natural. Rather than struggle to sustain awareness of awareness (which is another "doing"), simply be mindful as you continue with your day.

The most helpful way to practice resting in awareness is for brief moments, many times a day. If you approach this remembrance with curiosity and ease, you will find that you become increasingly drawn toward, and then at home in, the inner stillness of being.

TRUSTING THE GOLD

I had the recent blessing of witnessing my granddaughter Mia's birth. I sobbed as she was delivered, heart broken open at this ordinary and ever-astounding miracle. When we all settled and Mia was nursing contentedly in her mom's arms, I asked myself what my prayer was for her. It was that she trust her goodness. That she realize and trust the awareness, intelligence, and love that are intrinsic to her being.

Who knows what kind of personality Mia will develop, what challenges she will encounter in her health, her relationships, her learning, her world? If she can remember the goodness that lives in her and in all beings, she'll know true happiness. And not only that. She'll help serve the awakening of hearts in our world.

My prayer for Mia is my prayer for all of us. It's natural that we get caught in self-doubt, emotional reactivity, and ways of acting that cause separation and harm. We do this as individuals, and we turn against others—humans and other animals—on a societal level. And yet we are at a juncture in our unfolding as a species where we can purposefully evolve our own hearts and minds. We can cultivate mindfulness and self-compassion; we can learn to see past the mask of Unreal Others; we can Recognize and invite forward the gold in our own being and in others.

It helps to know that whatever you practice gets stronger. The more you practice RAIN and call on the four remembrances in daily life, the more familiar you'll become with openhearted awareness. In time you'll find that more than any habitual personality covering, this basic goodness feels like the truth of who you are.

It also helps to know that there are seasons to our awakening. Remember how the shadow god Mara continued to visit the Buddha after his enlightenment? The Buddha would respond with clarity and kindness: "I see you, Mara. Come, let's have tea." Just so, each time you meet difficulties with mindfulness and self-compassion, your confidence will grow. The old, limiting story of yourself no longer defines you. Even when challenging emotions arise, you can trust that you're basically okay. Then having tea with Mara becomes the gracious, good-humored, wise, and kind response to this human life.

Finally, remember that even when our lives seem most lonely, we're never on this path alone. We can't and don't awaken (or suffer) by ourselves. We are inextricably embedded in this web of living beings—always connected, always influencing each other, needing each other to mirror our goodness and remind us of our inherent potential.

As we close, I invite you to imagine a world where we humans see and trust and revere the gold within all beings.

Imagine how we'd help each other live true to ourselves, how we'd comfort and accompany each other, how we'd celebrate and create beauty together, how we'd awaken together and bring our collective care to our earth and to all beings everywhere.

We sow the seeds of radical compassion when we pause and say yes to what's here; when we turn toward love and rest in awareness. This cultivates the presence that guides us in living from compassion, in living true to our awakened heart.

May we continue to create the world we believe in together, and may the blessings of loving awareness extend endlessly in all directions.

APPENDIX 1
EVOLUTION OF THE
ACRONYM RAIN

ORIGINAL VERSION OF RAIN (MICHELE MCDONALD)

Recognize

Allow

Investigate

Non-Identification

CURRENT VERSION OF RAIN

Recognize

Allow

Investigate

Nurture

After the RAIN

I was introduced to the original version of RAIN in the late 1990s and taught it for a number of years. Along with many others, I was grateful to have an easy-to-remember mindfulness tool to guide me in untangling emotions.

During this time, I adapted RAIN in response to a key discovery in my own life: There is no healing without self-kindness. This was also evident in my students' experiences: "I know I'm supposed to be Investigating this shame, but I hate it . . . and I hate myself for having it." Realizing the necessity of self-compassion, I encouraged students to "Investigate with kindness," bringing an attitude of true interest, care, and friendliness to their inner lives.

My students were also having difficulty with the N—Non-identification. They'd regularly ask, "How do you *do* the step of Non-identification?" I had to explain that it wasn't actually a step. Rather, the R-A-I steps of RAIN awaken a full presence that transcends a limiting self-sense. Non-identification is not something we intentionally "do"; it is a state of being that emerges naturally.

The need for an active step of compassion and the confusion around Non-identification motivated me to change the acronym in 2014.

In its current version, the final step, Nurture, invites a full flowering of compassion. It creates a balancing of the two wings of mindfulness and heartfulness.

Non-identification is perceived most fully in After the RAIN. In the same way that the earth blossoms following a spring shower, after awakening through the four steps of RAIN you can simply rest in a naturally lucid and open presence. No longer identified with passing states like fear or anger, you discover the boundless, wakeful, and loving awareness that is your home.

The possibilities for RAIN continue to unfold as people explore using it in conflict resolution, clinical settings, and interpersonal meditations like RAIN Partners (see Appendix 2). Because RAIN awakens our most valued human capacities for wisdom and compassion, I hope many others will join in bringing these practices alive in our world.

APPENDIX 2

RAIN PARTNERS

Practicing with Others

My inspiration for RAIN Partners came from feedback given by people attending my weekend workshops. For years, I've guided participants in practicing RAIN in groups of four. They'd share at the beginning what they were going to work on and then debrief at the end with their challenges, insights, and openings.

Many have found this to be profoundly rewarding. I was struck in particular by reports from those already familiar with RAIN. They shared how the supportive presence of their partners deepened their inner work and how being together in a healing process forged authentic connection.

Their experience motivated me to create a format for RAIN that people could do on their own with partners, one that could be incorporated into their meditation practice and daily life. I'll share some key features of RAIN Partners here; if you would like to explore further, the full protocol and guided meditation

are available on my website: www.tarabrach.com/blog-rain
-partners-protocol.

WHAT ARE RAIN PARTNERS?

While RAIN can be done in small groups, for convenience
most people choose to work with a single partner. Your RAIN
partner might be a friend or family member, colleague, or
someone you don't know.

RAIN partners agree to do RAIN meditation sessions together on a regular basis—weekly, biweekly, monthly, or
whatever arrangement works. A session takes approximately
thirty-five to forty-five minutes and can be done in person, by
phone, or via the Internet. Continuing as partners over time
allows for a deepening of trust, safety, and mutual support.

ARE THERE PREREQUISITES TO BEING
A RAIN PARTNER?

Before participating as a RAIN partner, you and your partner should have your own regular mindfulness practices as
well as some experience working with RAIN. Each partner
should carefully review the guidelines in the protocol before
beginning.

WHAT HAPPENS IN A RAIN SESSION?

Both partners reflect in advance on a situation where they are getting caught in difficult emotions. It might be something triggered in a relationship, at work, by a health issue or an addictive behavior, or by events in our larger society. Each partner comes to the session with a particular situation in mind that activates the reactive pattern. You are advised not to choose something that is potentially traumatic or something that is highly charged and might be more than a peer process can hold in a healthy way.

As you'll see in the protocol, in the Recognize and Allow steps you and your partner will name aloud the challenging experience you are focusing on, while Investigate and Nurture are done in silence. You then return to a final sharing that will help you acknowledge what might have been difficult and clarify the insights or openings you most want to remember.

The protocol also includes essential guidelines (like confidentiality) that help you both create a safe and nourishing space for your RAIN sessions.

WHAT ARE THE BENEFITS?

Here, I'll share the words of students who have been RAIN partners:

- Having a partner makes me accountable. When I set up a RAIN session, I have to show up.

- It supports me in engaging fully with the process. When I'm alone, I sometimes start RAIN and then drift, or just stop. When I'm with my partner, I have to stick with it, go through all the steps. I'm always grateful.
- We call it our "RAIN dance" because together it's so much more powerful—and so beautiful in the way it connects us. Our presence brings out the best in each other.
- When we both are sharing problems, they feel less shameful and personal and unwieldy. It's much easier to be curious about what's going on inside me and to relate to myself with kindness.
- By exploring together what we learned, it seems to go deeper. And it sticks. I can remember through my week, and get so much from each time of practice.
- My partner helps me feel safe enough to explore issues I don't want to face on my own.
- This is empowering—I don't have to pay for a therapist or group . . . and get to do deep healing with someone who is along for the same ride!
- Doing this with a partner is a deep spiritual practice. By the end of a session, the little me has faded, and I'm left in a sense of "we," of openhearted awareness.
- When I do RAIN with a partner, I'm always struck by how the sense of "my problem" shifts. What starts out as a weighty difficulty that usually makes me feel bad about myself turns into something that feels unpleasant yet is held in a space of care.

We are always in relationship with our inner life and with each other. When we practice presence together, as we do with a RAIN partner, we co-create a field of radical compassion. This illuminates the truth of our connectedness and the intrinsic goodness that shines through ourselves and all beings.

For the RAIN Partners protocol and guided meditation, go to

www.tarabrach.com/blog-rain-partners-protocol/.

ACKNOWLEDGMENTS

The streams of inspiration, collaboration, and support that produced *Radical Compassion* feel like grace.

It's been my great good fortune to have Toni Burbank, a wonderful editor and friend, accompany me through three books. Toni's astute perspective and wise, loving companionship helped shape the project throughout.

My deep appreciation to my agent, Anne Edelstein, another dear one who has been right there by my side throughout these book-writing years with her enormous enthusiasm and savvy, and the support of her bright, warm heart.

Much gratitude to my initial Viking editor, Carole DeSanti, who saw the timeliness and value of a book aimed at widening the circles of compassion; and to my second Viking editor, Laura Tisdel, who has offered her vitality, vision, and consummate skill to bringing this book to the world.

Readers included my longtime friend and teaching partner, Jack Kornfield, and beloved sister, Darshan Brach. Their feedback directly enhanced the book's clarity, depth, and dimension.

And to my sister-friend Ruth King, a grateful bow for her wise and invaluable "mindful of race" mentoring.

Thanks to my assistants Janet Merrick, Barbara Newell, Christy Sharshel, and Léo Guillemin; and to retreat manager and fellow teacher La Sarmiento. Each of these dear friends has offered generous and loving support, bringing their whole hearts, creativity, and abundant skills to spreading dharma teachings.

I am blessed to have a great far-flung community of teaching friends and students who are devoted to awakening their hearts and serving others, and who continually inspire me with their courage, honesty, and sincerity in walking the spiritual path. My love and gratitude to my local IMCW *sangha*; to our Inclusivity, Equity, and Diversity Committee; to my White Awake training group, and my diversity *sangha*; to my global *sangha* of teacher-training participants and mentors; and to our ever-supportive friends and partners at Sounds True . . . to you all, it is a great delight to be on this adventure together.

A particular note of appreciation to those of you who were RAIN Partners during our pilot, and to the many who shared your RAIN stories with me . . . you have contributed immeasurably to bringing this book alive.

My gratitude for the brilliant contributions of Dan Siegel and Rick Hanson; for the inspiration of Van Jones, who awakens radical compassion through his activism and dialogues; for the groundbreaking work of Kristen Neff and Chris Germer in introducing mindful self-compassion to the world; and for the wisdom of dharma teacher Michele McDonald, who coined the original acronym RAIN.

I offer loving remembrance to my dear friend and fellow teacher Cheri Maples, whose courage and light touched countless lives. Cheri, dear . . . you are truly missed.

To my teachers past and present, my everlasting gratitude for reminding me of what I most cherish.

My heart is full with appreciation for my family: Narayan, Nicole, Mia, Betsy, Mady, Darshan, Peter and Ryan, and Alex. And to my live-in dear ones—Jonathan, my beloved husband, and kd, our indulged and darling pup—you bring the grace of good loving alive in countless fun, nourishing, and sweet ways. Thank you.